THE BEST IS YET TO COME

*Bro. Bill's Memories of Farm Life,
Family, and Faith*

WILLIAM R. WAMBSGANSS

Published by Legacy Press

Your life tells a story; we can help you write it.

www.legacypress.org

Printed in the United States of America

ISBN (softcover): 978-1-7342435-8-1

ISBN (eBook): 978-1-734235-9-8

Edited by Kendall Emmert at KendallEmmert.com

Cover and interior layout and design by Nelly Murariu at PixBeeDesign.com

TABLE OF CONTENTS

Foreword   v

1894-1940s

1.   Where It All Began: George and Eleanor   1
2.   The Family Grows   3
3.   Salvation Comes to the Farm   5
4.   Growing up on the Farm   10
5.   Truths of a Farm   14
6.   WWII: Fire at Home   16
7.   Spiritual Lessons from My Horses: Buster and Dick   18
8.   Paul's Surprise Appearance   20
9.   My Dad's Strong Character and Call into Ministry   22
10. Prayers of a Fifteen-Year-Old   25
11. Dead Ends and Wrong Turns   27
12. Bro. Curtis Thorpe   29
13. Bro. Burt Rutter: From Street Preaching to Church Pastoring   33
14. Bro. Art Wilson: My Second Father   36
15. Norma Luella Smith: Swept Off My Feet   38
16. First Time Pastor and Hamburger Gravy   41
17. Our Hive of B's   42
18. My Dad's Continual Call and Sacrifice   45
19. Praying and Playing   47
20. Car Wreck with Becky and Bonnie   50

1960s-1970s

21. My Call to Dodge City, Kansas   57
22. The Singing B's and Honey Too   60
23. Our Radio and Television Ministry   62
24. One of My Favorite Memories: Bob Morris   64
25. Don Smith: A Life Changed from Tragedy   65
26. The Big Flood   67

27. Go West Young Man   70

28. Bloom Youth Camp   72

29. Bro. Baker: Called to Serve in Haiti and Billy Loses Some Weight   73

30. Traveling to Europe in 1968   76

31. My Dad's Call to Bremerton, Washington   81

32. A Trip to the Holy Land with Norma   84

33. Blunders at the Bible Baptist Church   86

34. Bro. Bill Loves His Cars   87

1980s

35. Isaac Koppel's Gift   99

36. Dad's Homegoing   101

37. Following in Dad's Footsteps to Bremerton, Washington   104

38. Evelyn's Loss: Tony and Timmy Musgrove   107

39. Back to Haiti   110

40. Funny Baptism Stories   112

41. Lee Everett   114

1990s

42. Norma's Illness   119

43. Sharon Bates   121

44. To Haiti Again with Keith Bates   125

45. The Bates Family   127

46. Honorary Doctorates   128

47. Bible Schools and Youth Camps   129

48. Guest Speakers   131

Epilogue: Looking Through the Rearview Mirror   141

Publisher's Note   143

Appendix A: Obituary - William Richard Wambsganss   145

Appendix B: Where We Are Today - Blessed Beyond Measure!!!   153

Appendix C: Family Trees   157

FOREWORD

SHORTLY AFTER OUR UNCLE LEON passed away, his wife, Becky Wambsganss, called to tell us that her pastor had just brought a message about the children of Israel crossing the Jordan River. Joshua told one man from each of the twelve tribes to pick up a large stone out of the river, and pile them on the shore as a memorial, so that their children, in time to come, would not forget the works of God's mighty hand. Her pastor said that we should record the workings of God for our children as well.

Aunt Becky asked if dad would consider writing some of the wonderful memories of being raised in a godly Christian home. Thank you for the idea, Aunt Becky!

Our dad, "Bro. Bill" Wambsganss, currently lives in Austin, Texas with the oldest of his six children, Becky Lewis. Because of the COVID-19 pandemic of 2020, Becky was furloughed from her job as an aide for the Leander School District, so she and dad thought it would be a great time to start writing. Becky and dad spent two hours every single day, except Sundays, writing from six to eight a.m. most mornings. With Becky handwriting all of the stories, together, they filled up ten large journals.

Becky and dad asked all six of us kids to a "reading party." Becky read the stories aloud to us, crying most of the way through. Of course, we were crying too. We were so thrilled to have these stories from our beloved father! We knew most of them but to hear them one more time, through our dad's eyes, was priceless.

After we all gave dad the thumbs up, the books were handed over to Bill and Bonnie LaVielle (Bonnie is the second oldest). They took the ten handwritten journals and typed and organized them. Bill, Bonnie, and their children (three of which are schoolteachers) edited the stories, placing each section and chapter in order according to subject. With the help of Becky's daughter-in-law, Amberly Fowler, we found a Christian publisher and away we went.

This book has been such a labor of love for our dad and the six of us kids. Growing up as pastor's kids was such a blessing. Over the years, we have heard of pastor's kids that thought it was a burden, but we never thought that. Our dad was exactly the same at home as he was behind the pulpit. Our mom and dad were the godliest people we have ever known, and with every problem we had, dad and mom would get us together and pray about it. Raising children in a God-centered home is such a great heritage—what a blessing and what a great childhood we had!

The most important relationship we have in life is the one we have with the Lord and Savior, Jesus Christ. We hope this book will lead others to Him.

It is our prayer that this book will be a blessing to the people that read it,
Becky Lewis, Bonnie LaVielle, Brenda Rabe, Bill Wambsganss,
Beth Wambsganss, Betty Jo Methvin

Brother Bill and His Children

Give ear, O my people, to my law: incline your ears to the words of my mouth. I will open my mouth in a parable: I will utter dark sayings of old: Which we have heard and known, our fathers have told us. We will not hide them from their children, shewing to the generations to come the praises of the LORD, and his strength, and his wonderful works that he hath done. For he established a testimony in Jacob, and appointed a law in Israel, which he commanded our fathers, that they should make them known to their children: That the generation to come might know them, even the children which should be born; who should arise and declare them to their children: That they might set their hope in God, and not forget the works of God, but keep his commandments:

(PSALMS 78:1-7)

1894-1940s

Chapter 1

WHERE IT ALL BEGAN: GEORGE AND ELEANOR

BORN IN 1894 IN ALBUQUERQUE, New Mexico, my grandfather, Diamond Richard Smith, was the only survivor of three children. His father worked as a boiler maker on the old, steam engine for the Santa Fe Railroad. When my grandfather was young, the family moved to Lawrence, Kansas. As a teen, he accepted the Lord Jesus as his Savior and surrendered to preach the gospel. While pastoring the First Baptist Church in Colby, Kansas, he and my grandmother were married and God blessed them with a sweet baby, Eleanor Mae Smith. Soon after she was born, he enrolled at Ottawa University and became the pastor of the Baptist Church in Walnut, Kansas.

In 1918, as World War I concluded, the Spanish flu spread throughout the world and thousands died, including my grandparents and their newborn baby boy. The only family member to survive was their little girl, my mother, Eleanor, who was two-and-a-half years old. She was taken in by her grandparents, Mr. & Mrs. Phillip Cawthorne Smith.

The same flu epidemic hit my father's side of the family. He was five years old when his mother and his fifteen-year-old brother, Anton, died. My father and his twin brothers, Phillip and Earnest, and two sisters, Pauline and Ida, all survived. My grandfather's brother also died from the flu, leaving behind his wife Sophie and their daughter, Casilda. Sophie married my widowed grandfather, and they had a son named Merle. So, Sophie became my dad's aunt and stepmother.

Nine years later, tragedy would strike again when my mom's Grandmother Smith died. Her grandfather was in a desperate situation, so my mother was sent to live with two aunts in Pennsylvania. She lived there for a couple of years but returned to live with her grandfather and attend high school in Fall River, Kansas. They lived six miles in the country, so she would ride her horse, Buster, to school each day. She completed high school in three years and moved to Wichita, Kansas to attend business school. While she was there, the people she lived with took her to Olivett Baptist Church, where she accepted the Lord and was baptized.

After my mom graduated from business college, she returned to her grandfather and the farm. Her social life involved attending a weekly square dance at Glen Totten's barn a few miles down the road. It was there that she met the square dance caller, George William Wambsganss, who would one day be my father. There was an immediate interest between the two of them. Each week, my dad would ride his mule to the dances and my mother would ride her horse—the romance blossomed.

On September 20, 1934, at eighteen and twenty-one years of age, they borrowed Uncle Earnest's Model T and drove the many miles to Howard, Kansas, where they were married by the Justice of the Peace. My mother sold her prized violin for $15.00 to a neighbor on the farm to pay for the expenses of the wedding. After the ceremony, they walked across the street to a café for dinner and had a meal that cost thirty-five cents a plate. They returned to the farm and lived with Eleanor's Grandpa, Phillip Cawthorn (P.C.) Smith.

Chapter 2

THE FAMILY GROWS

O N JULY 4, 1935, I DISCOVERED AMERICA! My mother had been in hard labor, so our family doctor, who was over twenty miles away in Eureka, Kansas, was contacted to come and help deliver me. It was raining hard, the roads were very muddy, and the doctor's car got stuck. Dr. Francis Basham said my strong dad actually lifted the back end of the car over the ruts, so that he could get to the house.

Our home was an old house: no electricity, no phones, no indoor plumbing, TV, or radio. Our food was prepared on a wood burning stove. There were many things that old farmhouse did not have, but it had the most important one . . . loads of love!

When I was six months old, I became very ill with a severe ear infection and had to be rushed to have surgery at Wesley Hospital in Wichita, Kansas, sixty miles away. I was the youngest child to ever have the surgery in that hospital. As we were ready to leave the hospital, the doctor did a final check and began to cuss: I had it in the other ear as well!

It was in the middle of the depression and times were hard. During the next four months, my mother was able to live with the same friends she had lived with while in business school. For income, my dad stayed home trapping skunks and possums, so that he could sell the hides to Sears and Roebuck during the winter. He also chopped wood for $1.00/ day. While my dad stayed sixty miles away to work with my grandfather, my mother remained with me in Wichita at the hospital.

Later, my mom told me, each day she walked from her friend's house to the hospital in the bitter cold with shoes that had tops, but worn out soles. She recalled waiting for a traffic light to change, and when she picked up her feet to walk, her skin was frozen to the sidewalk. When she entered the hospital, she said she could hear me crying as soon as she opened the door.

I'm sure it was a great day for me and my parents when we finally got to go home. I don't remember it, but they never forgot it!

In 1938, when I was three years old, a bright ray of sunshine came our way with the blessing of my baby sister, Evelyn Marie. What a joy! She was the star of the show! My mother had a new project . . . to learn to make dresses on a Treddle sewing machine out of empty flour sacks. She hand-washed diapers and hung them on the line to dry. There was no such thing as store bought baby food: mother would chew the food and feed it to Evelyn.

Before long, Evelyn was walking, and could she ever talk! Who could have asked for more than our family of four? But then came the happy day when we learned another baby was on the way. I was six and Evelyn was three when the bundle from heaven came our way . . . but the doctor was called to make the long trip again. We both knew that mama was very sick, and when he arrived, he suggested that Evelyn and I go out to wait in the car. We weren't ready for what came next: daddy came out of the house with tears in his eyes and said that our little brother, Donald Phillip, had gone to heaven to be with Jesus!

He had been born with six fingers, six toes, and exposed organs. Our family was broken hearted but comforted because we knew we would enjoy him, with his perfect heavenly body, in heaven for eternity.

Chapter 3

SALVATION COMES
TO THE FARM

WHEN I WAS THREE YEARS OLD, an event changed the course of our family's history. A stranger stopped by while my dad was working in the field. He introduced himself as Pastor Rimer and invited us to a revival meeting at the Charleston Schoolhouse. My father told him that he had been baptized as a baby and that *his* church was as good as any. Cordially, he sent him away.

A few days later, the preacher returned and said, "I haven't seen you at the revival meeting." My father became agitated and said, "I guess I didn't make myself clear. I'm not coming to your meeting!" That time, he ran him off.

The preacher returned again and said, "I still haven't seen you at the revival meeting yet." My dad's conscience had been working on him about how stern he had been with Bro. Rimer. So this time he said, "If it means that much for me to come hear you preach after the way I treated you the other day, we will come hear you preach one time."

Dad, mom, Evelyn and I made the two-and-a-half-mile trip to the old schoolhouse, which had kerosene lamps for light, a wood burning, potbelly stove for heat, and school desks for chairs. This was the same school my mother had attended when she was a girl, and the one I would attend three years later. The funny thing is that my mother and I both rode the same horse, Buster, to that school. We ended up wearing him out after twenty years of taking us to school!

At the meeting, Bro. Rimer preached from John 3 where Jesus says, "Ye must be born again." Nothing you can do can pay your way to heaven. Jesus paid it all on the cross.

When we went home that night, my parents got down the big family bible and looked up John 3:7 and read, "Ye must be born again." They never attended the meeting again, but the words of the sermon continued to ring in my father's heart!

A few days later, we had trouble. The water pump used to water our cattle had broken. My Uncle Earnest came to help my father repair the well, and the very heavy pump and pipe had to be lifted many feet above the ground to get to the trouble. The device that held the pipe several feet in the air gave way, and the pump fell to the cement floor, smashing my Uncle Earnest's foot. My uncle was rushed to the doctor. Standing there, they shook realizing that if either one of them had been standing where the cast iron pump handle had fallen, they would have been killed.

While the doctor worked on my uncle's foot, my dad went out to the car feeling overwhelmed with conviction. He cried to the Lord and said, "If you'll forgive me of my sin, I'll accept you as my Savior." He experienced the joy of salvation and was 100% born again!

Miraculously, Uncle Earnest's foot completely healed, thank the Lord. From that very day, my dad's life was never the same. The first thing he wanted to do was find Bro. Rimer. After some searching, he found him several miles north of Charleston school, holding a meeting at another school. My father wanted to tell him the news that he had been saved!

Bro. Rimer rejoiced with him and said, "Now your sins are forgiven and heaven is your home. As a new believer your first steps of obedience are to be baptized in deep water, become a member of a local church, and make things right with your fellow man." He said that he needed to make it right with anyone that he had hard feelings toward. My dad didn't know what he meant and that he didn't think he had anyone like that in his life. And then he remembered he had a brother-in-law that he had told if he crossed his path, he would probably kill him. Bro. Rimer said, "George, you shouldn't feel that way." My dad told him it wasn't his fault, that his brother-in-law had beat him out of $15.00 on a mowing machine. Bro. Rimer told my dad that he needed to ask his brother-in-law for forgiveness because of the way he was feeling towards him.

My dad asked Bro. Rimer to go with him to talk to his brother-in-law, and they went together. My father told his brother-in-law that he had accepted Jesus as his Savior and that he was sorry for the way he treated him. After Bro. Rimer and my father left, the brother-in-law said to one of dad's brothers, "George has something we don't have!" From that point on, my dad and his brother-in-law were great friends.

My father followed the Lord in baptism, and things were never the same in our house after that. We no longer worked on Sundays, and one of our neighbors said, "What's happened to George? I don't hear him cussing his horses anymore."

After my dad was saved, Brother Rimer continued to visit our farm. As a little boy, being with our pastor was like being in the presence of an angel! We should only have one main hero: Jesus. But right under Jesus were our pastors! We sure did love all of them and knew they loved us!

Bro. Rimer and his family knew what it was to walk by faith. Their large family was willing to live in deep poverty so that country folk like us could hear the gospel. Bro. Rimer's family would get permission to live in a vacant house and they would just trust the Lord for their food. They would kind of campout.

Sometimes, Bro. Rimer would come by and pick up my daddy in his old car, and they would go out to invite people to a schoolhouse revival and talk to them about the Lord. Sometimes, the father of the family would need a haircut and, since Bro. Rimer was a barber by trade, he would give him a haircut

One day, when dad was out with Bro. Rimer on visitation, he asked the preacher, "How's your gasoline?" Bro. Rimer said it was empty and, soon after that, a family they visited asked him the same question. The man had five gallons of gasoline and put it in Bro. Rimer's car. Down the road, someone would have a chicken and a box of eggs, insisting on sending the food home with our pastor. Eventually, he went home to be with the Lord after being a missionary in Mexico. His whole life was one that was lived for the Lord and lived by faith.

On another day, Bro. Rimer and my father were out witnessing and won a farmer to the Lord. When they got back to town, they were told he was one of the worst drunkards in the county. That sinner, saved by grace, grew in the Lord and became very faithful in the church. My father was always a good testimony and witnessed to his siblings and his whole family. They knew he loved the Lord.

Our pastors and their families were always our best friends. When we would butcher a cow, they would always be given a large portion. It was not uncommon for our pastor to show up for a visit early in the morning and share our huge farmer's breakfast. He never needed to have an invite and knew he was always welcome. He also enjoyed going fishing and hunting with us. It was a great time for him to unwind.

We would always accompany our pastor to various preachers' meetings. In those days, we would not stay in motels but in church members' homes. It was a time of great Christian hospitality. When one of our pastors would resign, our whole family was so sad and we didn't want them to go.

A tiny church in Fredonia, Kansas called Bro. Rimer to be their pastor. One of our neighbors, the Austins, took us the twenty-five miles to church in Fredonia every Sunday, until they moved and then we went on our own.

My parents remained so faithful serving the Lord. My! How He blessed them! Soon my father was able to buy a 160-acre farm, and we didn't have to rent anymore. Every time the church doors were open, we were there. Dad always tithed on every dollar of income he ever made. He never worked on Sunday other than feeding and milking cows and other animal chores.

I also remember how my dad laughed a lot, was always the life of the party, and such a hard worker. I've never seen a woman more loyal to the Lord, her husband, and family than my mother. All the hardships in her life never made her bitter, just better! I don't know how I could have been more blessed.

We attended the church in Fredonia from 1938-1953, when my father and I both went into full-time ministry as pastors. Those were wonderful years when scores of people were saved and lives were changed.

Even so, I know the best is yet to come . . . when all the family are saved and together forever in heaven: no pain, no sorrow, no fears and no tears!

Chapter 4

GROWING UP ON
THE FARM

Let your conversation be without covetousness;
and be content with such things as ye have: for he hath said,
I will never leave thee, nor forsake thee.

(HEBREWS 13:5)

FARM HOURS BEGAN AT SUNRISE and farm life didn't end until way after dark. We didn't have TV or radio, so we were always in bed by nine o'clock.

Almost all of our food supply was raised and provided by our own farm. We had very little money and were very poor, but we didn't know it because everyone else was poor too. We worked hard! We didn't worry about the stock market and the economy, we just joyously trusted the Lord and He always saw us through. We were oh-so-happy!

Back in those days, you would mail order baby chicks as either pullets, roosters, or a mixed run, and they would be delivered by the mailman to your door. They came 100 in a box and if you missed him, he would return them to the Post Office to be picked up. It really was thrilling watching the mother hen and how she protected her baby chicks.

A day on the farm consisted of feeding chickens, gathering eggs (the hens would lay them everywhere), feeding pigs, milking cows, putting the milk in ten-gallon milk cans, and sitting them out on the road for the milk truck to pick up and take to the Longhorn Cheese Factory. This all had to be done before we caught the bus to school. We would milk the cows and separate the milk in the old cream separator and pour it in a big bowl. Milk would come out of one spout and cream another. A five-gallon milk can containing cream would be taken to town and sent by railroad to be sold in Wichita, Kansas. Then they would send the empty cans back for us to re-fill.

Breakfast consisted of eggs, cornmeal mush, pork chops, and, occasionally, oatmeal. Can you imagine this? When the baby chicks were grown, we had fried chicken every day. Then for supper, it would be tomato soup or potato soup. In the middle of winter, a special dessert treat was homemade ice cream. We had our own milk, cream, and eggs, and would break the ice off of the cow's water tank—it was delicious! My dad and mom always had a garden, so vegetables were plentiful too.

Money wasn't plentiful in those days, but neighboring was. Farmers would trade work with each other rather than pay money. The host farmer's wife would prepare a meal like you wouldn't believe. It got to be a competition to see who could outdo the previous family.

My father owned a threshing machine (these were days before combines were invented). The threshing machine would be parked in the field. A few weeks earlier, a binder machine would have gone through the field and cut wheat or oats, leaving behind bundles all over the field. On harvest day, wagons pulled by a team of horses would gather up the bundles and bring them to the threshing machine. The machine would pitch them into a large conveyor and out the other end would come straw, building a large straw stack. The grain was caught to be stored in the barn.

As a child, each one of us had chores to do, such as feed the pigs, gather the eggs, lock the hen house, and so forth. But when I was seven years old, I started on the harvest crew. My job was to take a glass gallon jug filled with water from wagon to wagon for the workers to drink. They would give me a penny or two, and on a good day, a nickel! In those days we weren't germ conscious, so all the men drank from the same jug. Thank the Lord we survived!

Sometimes, as a little boy, I would get busy playing, and when we would sit down to eat supper my father would ask if I had done my chores.

I would shamefully admit that I hadn't, and he would tell me to go out and do them.

By that time, it was dark, and I was afraid: I could imagine a boogeyman behind every one of the tall trees. In my heart, I was scared to death! There's nothing worse than being alone in the dark! I must admit, there *were* times I could walk in the darkest night among those same trees and wasn't at all afraid. My secret was that I had my big, brave, six-foot-tall dad walking with me and holding my hand.

Now years later, my father is in heaven and my heavenly father walks with me through the darkest nights. I am so thankful for his presence!

There was nothing like watching the sunrise and the beautiful sunset! There were also storms, lightening, thunder, hail, rain, and afterward a gorgeous rainbow. Oh, the joy and peace of being alone working in the field and seeing the mama hen and baby chicks, the sow and her piglets, the cow and the little calves, the pony and her cute, little colt; watching the wild baby rabbits, the squirrels in the trees, and tiny birds with their mother in a soft nest . . .

From age eleven through high school, I spent most of my spare time plowing, driving a tractor, and working in the field with horses. Those were some of the greatest times of my life. I would spend time alone, just me and my Lord, singing, praying, preaching, and memorizing scripture. My congregation was the cows, horses, and squirrels. We worked six days a week, but never on Sunday, even in harvest; we never had a harvest hailed-out, even though other nearby farmers did. I attribute it to my dad always putting the Lord first with church attendance and tithing.

It was a time to think, to be thankful, to meditate, to pray, to plan, to sing, and dream. Oh what precious memories—to be alone with the Lord! They were some of the greatest times of my life.

I was blessed with my parents' love and their great examples and prayers. I was blessed beyond measure listening to my Grandfather PC Smith's exciting stories—he was the world's best storyteller!

What wonderful memories I have of growing up on the farm. So many lessons learned about how to trust God in every situation. During the good times and bad, it's so wonderful to see how God provides.

I am thankful I grew up before there were so many outside influences that our kids have today. It was not time wasted; it was a time God invested in us. Every step was ordered by the Lord.

Chapter 5

TRUTHS OF A FARM

About Seeds:
*Be not deceived; God is not mocked: for whatsoever a man
soweth, that shall he also reap. For he that soweth to his
flesh shall of the flesh reap corruption; but he that soweth to
the Spirit shall of the Spirit reap life everlasting.*

(GALATIANS 6:7-8)

ONE OF THE MOST THRILLING TIMES growing up was the planting of crops, the sewing of seeds. It was only surpassed by the joy of the harvest. But before seeds were sown, there first had to be the preparation of the soil.

*For thus saith the LORD to the men of Judah and
Jerusalem, Break up your fallow ground, and sow not
among thorns.* **(JEREMIAH 4:3)**

Oh, the anticipation of a thriving field growing day by day, the smell of freshly toiled sod, and the dream of what it will become through faith! A person can envision a great outcome, but hard work is also involved: seeds must be watered, weeds must be pulled. And weeds . . .weeds never need to be planted; they just grow on their own, taking over if they aren't eradicated.

One thing is for sure: the seed you sow is what you will reap. You can't sow to sin and the world expecting to reap the smile of the Lord and His blessings. If you live by the Holy Spirit, you will reap joy and a spiritual life for eternity.

About the Harvest:

Because sentence against an evil work is not executed
speedily, therefore the heart of the sons of men is fully set in
them to do evil. **(ECCLESIASTES 8:11)**

But if ye will not do so, behold, ye have sinned
against the Lord: and be sure your sin will find you out.
(NUMBERS 32:23)

The harvest doesn't come immediately after the seeds are sown and God doesn't pay every Saturday night. The Bible says that you can expect to reap much more than you sow. Whether you live for the Lord or live for the flesh, which is yourself. But also remember that in a time of growth, there will come storms in life. Some will be severe, but if you are walking with the Lord, you can be assured that Jesus will be with you during the worst hurricane in your life—the Lord will never leave you or forsake you! When that storm is over, you will look up and see His beautiful rainbow of promise. He's a friend that sticks closer than a brother.

Yet, how dreadful is the harvest for the one who has lived their life for Satan and themselves to reap and suffer eternal separation from God and heaven. In the Bible, God assures us that he is not willing that any should perish, but all would come to repentance.

So tell me my friend, are you looking forward to *your* harvest?

Chapter 6

WWII:
FIRE AT HOME

*Someday all of us will stand before God at the Judgement
Seat of Christ, and all we will have to offer to the Lord is
smoldering coals and a cloud of smoke, because we have only
lived our lives for this world and self.*

—BRO. BILL

O N DECEMBER 7, 1941, the United States experienced a tragic attack
on Pearl Harbor by Japan. We were already at war with Germany
and Italy which would be known as World War II. We were suddenly
brought to our knees not knowing if we would win or lose. Fathers and
sons were drafted into the army to fight, and women went to work man-
ufacturing ammunition and weapons for the Great War. Everyone was
busy gathering scrap metal to be used in the war effort. Most families
had at least one member of the family who was serving in the military.

Church attendance flourished and brokenhearted prayer meetings
were the new norm. Living on the farm, our form of communication was
our weekly *Kansas City Star* newspaper. The paper would also list blackout
dates, which meant we would have to put paper over the windows. We
were told that even an aircraft would be able to see a candle in the window
from miles and miles away. Food was in short supply, and we were issued
ration books from the government for food, flour, sugar, meat, tires for
cars, etc.

In the middle of the war, my mother became pregnant. Because her previous pregnancy ended with Donnie's deformity and stillbirth, she went to stay with our dear friends in Eureka to be closer to the doctor.

The big day came on February 25, 1944, and Leon George was born. There's an old saying that all smart people are born in February, and Leon sure validated it! We became a happy family of five during a time of national uncertainty.

Ten years had passed since my parents had married, and I remember that my dad worked from very early in the morning until dark. We had a nice house and much to show for his hard work. One day, when Leon was six months old, and I was walking home from school with Evelyn and a couple of friends, I thought I heard geese flying overhead, but one of my friends said it was someone screaming. I looked a half mile over the trees and saw clouds of smoke coming out of the top of our house, realizing that the voice was my mother crying for help!

When mom washed clothes, she had to heat the water in a tub set on top of a fuel oiled cook stove, which must have boiled over and started the fire. Mother ran through the flames to get Baby Leon out of the house, but Leon's face was burned. A friend drove my mother and Leon to the doctor in Fredonia.

Although many neighbors responded when they saw the smoke, the house was a total loss, except the garage, where we lived for months. With the help of neighbors, my dad took a long pole and knocked down the brick chimney, the only thing left standing, so that it would not fall on someone and hurt them.

As my father looked and saw ten years of his life gone, he had tears in his eyes. All that was left of that hard work was a pile of smoldering coals and a cloud of smoke. All of our material riches were totally gone.

During that same year, while I was working with a team of horses in a field four miles out of town, I heard whistles blowing and bells ringing. I knew it must mean that the war was over! It was 1945 and I was ten years old. What a happy day!

Chapter 7

SPIRITUAL LESSONS FROM MY HORSES: BUSTER AND DICK

*Trust and obey, for there's no other way to be
happy in Jesus, but to trust and obey.*

—SONG LYRICS FROM "TRUST AND OBEY"

WRITTEN BY JOHN H. SAMMIS

I WAS MORE PRIVILEGED than most kids raised on a farm, because I had my own personal horse, Buster. He was as gentle a pony as you could imagine and very obedient. I learned a great spiritual lesson from him.

There is a love affair between a cowboy and his horse: the cowboy provides food, water, and protection for his horse and, in turn, his horse longs to please his master and make him happy. Farmers used to say that a horse was no good until it was broke. Somewhere in the life of the horse, this change takes place. I don't know who broke my horse, Buster, but they sure did a good job. I never had a better animal friend than my horse, Buster. He died at twenty-one years old.

You may ask, "What does it mean for a horse to be broke?" It basically means to let his rider be the boss. If left to himself, a horse will insist on doing his own thing. But if he is to be useful, his stubborn will has to be broken. The Bible tells us that we are all born with a sinful nature and that our will must be broken so that our Master may be in control. Like Jesus said to God the Father, "Not my will, but thine be done."

One day, my father got all of us guys together, and we drove our cattle to pasture several miles away. The horse I got was named Dick and was one of my father's best work horses. He was great at driving cattle, but was also very feisty.

The next day after church, my father and mother drove the car up to the pasture to count the cows and see if any had gotten out. My parents were not yet home, and the milk cows had to be milked, so I decided to take Dick to round them up.

Now, I was able to corral Dick, but I had to lead him to a feed bunk because he was too tall for me to mount from the ground. He was stubborn and would not come alongside the feed bunk, standing at an angle which made it difficult for me to get on him. Finally, out of desperation, I jumped to get on him. My leg was over his back and I was hanging and holding onto his bridle, but he started running. When I couldn't hold on anymore, I fell to the ground, but he ran on. Somehow, I was able to make it the 500 feet back to the house.

When my parents arrived home, they found me semi-conscious. When we arrived at the hospital, fifty miles away, they evaluated me and said that I had a concussion and a broken left shoulder. Bruises covered my body. For the next six weeks, I was flat on my back in the hospital with traction ropes and pulleys and weights shifting in various directions so that the bones could heal.

Once again, my mother stayed by my side until I was released from the hospital, just like she had when I was a baby with my mastoid surgery. I'm thankful for such loving, godly parents. I don't know how the rest of the family made it with mother being there with me, but they did. I guess I was a mess! But most of all, my Heavenly Father was sure watching over me.

My dad took Dick, his very best work horse, to the auction and sold him because of me. He said he would never be able to trust him again. My parents and my God were always there when I needed them.

In this day of absentee fathers, I'm so glad mine was always there for me, and he always set a good example. When my time comes to die, I hope that I will have lived to please my dearest friend, my master and my Lord, Jesus Christ and not myself. I long to hear him say, "Well done good and faithful servant!"

Chapter 8

PAUL'S SURPRISE APPEARANCE

IT WAS A NORMAL WEEKEND on the farm, but that particular Saturday evening my mother became violently ill and feared a previously removed tumor had reoccurred. My father and I rushed her the sixty miles to Eureka, Kansas to Dr. Basham, our family doctor, where he immediately prepared her for surgery.

My father and I anxiously waited and prayed in the waiting room on the first floor. The nurse came out of my mother's room on the second floor, telling the nurses in the hallway, "This woman's not having surgery, she's having a baby!"

A little while later, the doctor came to our floor and told my dad to sit down. My father's first thought was that mother had died, but then he broke the news: "You're the father of a new baby boy!" Dad was shocked with unbelief. He said, "Doctor can't you tell when a lady's pregnant? What kind of doctor are you?" Dr. Basham replied, "I normally can, but she has complained for eighteen months and this is the first time I've had a baby take that long to get here!"

The previous week my dad's stepmother had asked my mom if she was pregnant again, but my mom had replied that it was just that "old tumor come back."

I walked across the street from the hospital to a little café, and guess what I heard playing on the juke box? Stuart Hamblen's song, *It Is No Secret What God Can Do.* What fitting words for what we had just experienced!

On February 4, 1950, I met my youngest brother, Paul Francis Wambsganss. I guess my dad wasn't too mad at the doctor because Paul was named after Dr. Francis Basham! My parents would often say that day was one of the happiest days of their lives! On the way home from the hospital, we had to drive twenty miles to Toronto, Kansas to borrow diapers from cousins, Ed and Glena Ward, who recently had a new baby. When we got back home, church members, friends, and family members insisted that my mom had known all along and just kept it a secret. They wondered how a woman could be pregnant and not know it.

Thank God for this precious bundle of joy he dropped on us that day. Our family was now complete.

Chapter 9

MY DAD'S STRONG CHARACTER AND CALL INTO MINISTRY

Bring ye all the tithes into the storehouse . . . and prove me now herewith, saith the Lord of hosts, if I will not open the windows of heaven, and pour out a blessing, that there shall not be room enough to receive it.

(MALACHI 3:10)

THROUGHOUT THE YEARS, what God said in this verse has proven to be true! Just as I could never outgive my father, neither have I been able to outgive my heavenly father. He owns the cattle on a thousand hills. The wealth of the world is his. The Psalmist said, "Once I was young, but now I am old, and I've never seen the righteous forsaken or his seed begging bread" (Psalm 37:25).

I never knew a harder worker on the farm than my dad, and I never knew a man that loved the Lord more than my dad. There is an old saying, *you can take a boy off the farm, but you can't take the farm out of the boy.* That was true for the thirty years of dad's pastoring. He raised a garden in every place he pastored and took a milk cow to his first church in Toronto, Kansas. And even at his last church in Bremerton, Washington, he had pigs, chickens, and a garden in his backyard. The morning he went to heaven, he had just been out picking green beans.

He that winneth souls is wise.

(PROVERBS 11:30)

God was faithful and blessed my dad all through his life. Everything my father put his hand to he did with all his heart. When he worked hard and when he played hard, he gave it his all. He never finished 8th grade because he was needed on the farm. My dad excelled in Bible study and preaching and was well versed in the scriptures. He was as honest and generous as the day is long. Even though he was not perfect, he was the best man a dad could be.

Dad's call to the ministry was certainly dramatic. My three-year-old brother, Leon, was left at the house with my grandfather, while the rest of us went out picking blackberries. When we came back to the house, Leon had ingested a can of kerosene that my grandfather had kept by our wood burning stove. My parents quickly put him in the car and headed to our doctor, about twenty miles away in Eureka, Kansas.

About halfway to the hospital, Leon passed out and a terrible thing happened . . . we got a flat tire. My father flagged down the next car that came by and begged them to take my mother and brother to the doctor, while my dad fixed the flat tire. Dr. Basham pumped Leon's stomach, but told dad he didn't know if Leon would be alive in the morning or not.

Several weeks prior to this accident, God had been speaking to my dad about surrendering to preach. No one else was aware of this. During that night, God spoke to my dad's heart and seemed to say, "If you want to see Leon alive tomorrow morning, surrender to my call for your life." The following Sunday, George Wambsganss made it public to the church that God had called him to preach and, thank the Lord, Leon made a full recovery.

In dad's preaching, you could always tell he was a farmer. Many of his illustrations and stories would sound like, "you reap what you sow," and "sow not among thorns" or "break up the fallow ground," and so on.

He was always very black and white; either something was right or it was wrong. Right should be rewarded, and wrong should be punished. Because of that, I knew what it was like to be spanked and/or corrected in other ways. Two things he hated more than any other was a thief and a liar. In other words, dishonesty! Not only was he a very hard working and honest man, he was very generous and fair in his dealings.

Once a year, my father would hire a man with a big truck and load up our yearling calves to sell at the stockyards, riding with the driver many miles away to Kansas City. It was like our family's once a year payday! I remember as a child in the first grade, I couldn't wait for my dad to return home with a special gift for me. I remember getting a brown pair of pants with an orange stripe down the side, a pair of rubber boots, and a metal toy airplane.

Throughout my life, he and my mother were always so giving. Whether it was a birthday, Christmas, or a just-because-day, they always thought of others. The Bible says, "It's more blessed to give than to receive!"

As I grew older, even though my resources were limited, I found joy in trying to follow his example by giving gifts to my parents and others. The older I got, the more expensive my gifts to my father became. As years passed by, I wanted to try and outgive my father, but it proved to be impossible.

One year in Dodge City, after a long time pastoring there, I gave my father a very nice briefcase. By then, we had a nice church building and a room I called my office. My father came to visit and I don't remember what the occasion was, but he said, "Let's go buy you some office furniture." He bought me a beautiful desk, an office chair, a bronze desk lamp, and drapes for the windows. Once again, I was convinced that there was no way I could outgive my father and, throughout life, I have also learned that I cannot outgive my heavenly father.

While pastoring near that naval base in Bremerton, Washington, my dad delighted in taking Navy boys out hunting. These young men had been raised in New York City, or similar areas, so hunting was very foreign to them. They had never experienced anything like that.

Since he met the Lord, the lifelong desire of my father was to win souls. A song writer wrote, "We will come rejoicing bringing in the sheaves." And that's just what he did . . . just after picking beans. There were many people who had been saved during his faithful ministry. What a great reunion that must have been when they met together with their Savior in heaven!

Chapter 10

PRAYERS OF A FIFTEEN-YEAR-OLD

ONE OF MY FAVORITE SUNDAY school teachers a was a little bitty lady named Virginia Duncan. She could make Bible stories come to life! I'm sure she played a big role in my love of children's work. So, at fifteen, when I was asked to teach a ten-year-old boys' Sunday school class, I decided to do it. What a great opportunity to invest in these boys.

Little did I know that nine years later, one of the boys from my Sunday school class would be my right-hand man for twenty-two-and-a-half years at the church I would pastor in Dodge City, Kansas. Richard Buchanan was my music man, treasurer, and MC on our weekly TV broadcast. He was a true friend to *this* pastor.

One year, as a member of *The Happy Hustlers 4-H Club*, my project was raising a baby pig. Much to my surprise, I won the blue ribbon at the 4-H fair and was even able to sell my prize pig for a thrilling $74.00! I took the money to the local hardware store and bought a beautiful new bicycle. It was my prized possession.

I would ride my bike back and forth, four miles to town, and one time to a revival meeting nine miles away in Altonia, Kansas. On Sunday, I would get up early and ride to the homes of my school friends and wake them up for Sunday school. There were no Sunday school bus routes in those days—but this was my personal bike route!

Other thrilling memories of me and my bicycle were those of visiting families, inviting them to church, and witnessing to them about the Lord, including Walt Reinhardt and his wife. My dad had hired him on a few occasions to bring his bulldozer out to push trees and build ponds. After inviting Walt to a revival meeting, I earnestly prayed that he would come to the meeting. At the end of that service, I looked up and Walt was at the altar accepting Jesus as his Savior.

Later, Bro. Kenneth Bowen, who was pastoring our church in Fredonia, went to a meeting in Wichita, Kansas, and took Bro. Walt with him. After the meeting, they went to a Christian bookstore and the pastor bought $85.00 worth of study books. Bro. Walt insisted on paying for them saying, "Pastor, let me pay for them. The last time I was in Wichita I spent more than that on liquor!"

Isn't it amazing that God hears and answers the prayers of teenagers? What a transformation took place in Walt's life; what a blessing when the Lord changed him!

Chapter 11

DEAD ENDS AND
WRONG TURNS

There is a way which seemeth right unto a man,
but the end thereof are the ways of death.

(PROVERBS 14:12)

WHEN I WAS SIXTEEN YEARS OLD, I was able to do a man's work on the farm: feed cattle, work in the field with a team of horses, buck bales of hay, as well as tractor plowing in the fields.

Not only did my father and I work together, but we also played together. One day after taking care of cattle in the pasture and walking back to the house, we went by the watering pond where the cattle drank water. My dad started wrestling with me trying to throw me in the water. All of a sudden he said, "Stop, stop, I've got a bad pain in my stomach." He ended up having his gallbladder removed sixty miles away in Eureka, Kansas at the nearest hospital. After that, I would jokingly tell him, "That will teach you not to wrestle with me."

My mother stayed with my dad at the hospital, and I was left on the farm to do the chores and watch my siblings. One afternoon, after all the work was done, I decided to take the old Ford pickup with the kids, drive to Eureka, and visit dad in the hospital. Even though it had been raining quite heavily, I decided to take the back way through Toronto. About fifteen miles from home, I came to a dead-end road and couldn't remember which was the right way. I decided to turn left, which turned out to be the wrong direction. The longer I drove, the more the gravel road turned into mud. There were cattle all around us in the pasture and it was getting dark. We were stuck in the mud and there was no way to turn around and go back.

I didn't know what to do, but since I had to do something, I told the kids to stay in the pickup so that I could walk and try to find help. What a frightful time it was! Finally, down the road, I saw a house in the distance.

When I arrived, I was relieved to discover the family had a phone. I called my cousin, Ed Ward, in Toronto. The man told my uncle where we were, and my cousin said he would come and rescue us. After I got off the phone, the kind people told me that it was good we had gotten stuck, because not far down the road there was a bridge that had washed out and it could have been disastrous!

My cousin found his way to where we were and got us out of the mud and headed in the right direction. Late that night, we arrived at the hospital safe and sound to see my father.

Thank the Lord for his watch care over us. We thought we were on the right road, but we had made a wrong turn. We all need to be sure that we are headed to our heavenly home: the right way.

> *Jesus saith unto him, I am the way, the truth and the life:no man cometh unto the Father, but by me.* **(JOHN 14:6)**

> *Neither is there salvation in any other: for there is none other name under heaven given among men, whereby we must be saved.* **(ACTS 4:12)**

When we know we're on the right road to our heavenly home we can say, along with the apostle Paul,

> *For to me to live is Christ, and to die is gain.*
> **(PHILIPPIANS 1:21)**

For the child of God who knows that he's on the right road to heaven, the end of that road, our death, is not to be feared, but is to be looked forward to. We will be safe at home with Jesus forevermore!

Chapter 12

BRO. CURTIS THORPE

All through my life, God has been so good to me
and kept his promise: And I will give you pastors
according to mine heart.

(JEREMIAH 3:15)

OUR NEXT PASTOR WAS NO STRANGER to living by faith. He was saved out of the oil fields of west Texas and answered God's call to preach, leaving the good money of oil. He attended Bible Baptist seminary of Fort Worth, Texas. When he graduated from seminary, he was called to pastor our struggling church in Fredonia, Kansas. Bro. Curtis Thorpe, his wife Dorothy, and their two sons, Jerry and Paul Riley, experienced a life of sacrifice doing the Lord's work.

My, how the Lord did bless! Souls were saved and we also grew in the Lord. One day, Bro. Thorpe and my dad were way out in the country soul-winning, and they knocked on Berl Gray's door and won him to the Lord. When they got back to town, they were told that the man was one of the worst drunks in the area.

Berl Gray's life was transformed and he attended church each Sunday. He donated trees from off his farm for lumber to build onto our church house. He would take Bro. Thorpe and my dad out on the river fishing with him, and when he would get thirsty, he would just drink water right out of the river. But my dad and Bro. Thorpe thought that, compared to what he used to drink, that surely couldn't hurt him!

Bro. Thorpe, his son, Jerry, my father, and I would go on all-night fishing trips on the Fall River. You wouldn't believe the picnic my mother would send with us. We would eat it all night after we set out trout lines and bank lines. Once we were sure that all the lines were baited, we'd eat and relax. After, it would be time to run the lines, take off the fish that we caught, and re-bait the hooks. This went on all night.

It was a sad day for our family and the whole church when Bro. Thorpe told us he was leaving. He had accepted the pastorate for a church in Odessa, Texas. I remember that I had his picture sitting on my dresser in my bedroom, and I remember how sad I was to hear that they were leaving.

My father and several men of the church told him he was out of God's will. They told Bro. Thorpe they didn't think the Lord was through with him at our small church. We planned a big going away party for him, but when we arrived, the Thorpe's weren't there. Later, Bro. Thorpe said that he knew that if he had stayed for the party, he would have never left. But the Lord knew what he was doing, and he had plans for our church in Fredonia, Kansas.

Despite what we had wanted, God used Bro. Curtis Thorpe and his son Jerry to build the largest congregation in Odessa, Texas. We would attend national fellowship meetings, and I couldn't wait to see Bro. Thorpe. Our family went to visit them in Odessa about a year after they left Fredonia. I experienced my first visit to Dairy Queen! I have never gotten over my love for the Thorpe family or Dairy Queen ice cream!

Bro. Curtis Thorpe and my father are now in Heaven, but Jerry Thorpe and I remain friends here on earth.

Pastors have meant so much to me over the years. Bro. Kenneth Bowen, Burt Rutter, Bob Perryman, Homer Quinlan, Harold Elder, Art Wilson, Dave Brown, Richard Green and Steve Ledbetter and so many other preacher friends have meant the world to me and my family.

Pastor means shepherd . . . what a loving relationship. Our pastors were indeed true disciples of Jesus.

1950s-1960s

Chapter 13

BRO. BURT RUTTER: FROM STREET PREACHING TO CHURCH PASTORING

A FEW MONTHS BEFORE BRO. Rutter came to our church, I had gone forward in church to share my decision to follow God's calling and surrender to preach. Bro. Thorpe had asked the congregation if anyone was surprised!

Now, our new pastor, Bro Burt Rutter, told my dad that since God had also called him to preach, then he needed to preach. Almost immediately, Bro. Rutter started taking us out on Saturdays to preach on the streets. My father bought a new 1951 Plymouth and a public announcement system with two big horn speakers that sat on top of the car. The PA system was powered off the 6-volt car battery. In those days, there was a country village every few miles where the railroad crews would live and shop. They would get paid every Friday night, so everyone would go shopping on Saturday. The streets were lined with people, and stores would stay open as long as people would shop.

We had captive audiences to witness to in towns and villages all across Kansas: Altonia, Toronto, Buckston, Severy, New Albany, Howard, Eureka, and Neodasha. Every Saturday, we would go to three of these towns, park the car, and start playing gospel songs on the PA system, then one of us would preach while the others would pass out tracts and witness. This would be repeated until all three of us had preached.

Some would stop and listen. Occasionally, you would hear an amen or a cat call. Some teenagers would try to dance to the music in the street. Then, we would turn the speakers around so they wouldn't catch the wind and go to the next village. We would repeat the same format until we had been to all three places.

We lived for those Saturdays when we could go out and preach. We had all kinds of experiences, including good Christians who appreciated it and drunks who heckled us. Thank the Lord a few people were saved, only the Lord knows how many. We were thrilled to get a lot of practice preaching, as well as memories that have lasted a lifetime and maybe into eternity.

If we remembered all the experiences of that street preaching, it would fill a book. Thank the Lord for all the faithful pastors and Christians who invested in our lives.

Toronto was one of our favorite towns to preach on the streets. Two uncles and aunts of ours also lived there, along with several cousins. Some of them would attend services. It was about twenty miles north of Fredonia. It wasn't long before we started having services there on Sundays in order to get a church started. Dad bought a house there, and we moved with one milk cow. It was our first house with indoor plumbing. I attended my senior year of high school there also. We drove back and forth each day to do the farm work.

We rented the American Legion Hall on Main Street in Toronto for services. We would go in really early Sunday mornings to clean up beer cans and cigarette butts from the night before. Then we would go around and pick up kids for the services.

After we gained the experience of preaching on the streets, Bro. Rutter felt led of the Lord that my father and I should be ordained. So, at a fellowship meeting in May 1952, we were! I was sixteen years old, and my father was thirty-nine.

In the middle of that winter, Westside Baptist Church in Emporia, Kansas called my dad to be their pastor. My dad sold his house in Toronto to a brother-in-law. He asked his brother Merle to take over the farm in a partnership, so he could spend his time pastoring. So that I could finish my senior year, I lived with an aunt and uncle and stayed in Toronto.

The Emporia church was meeting in a basement and, while there, my dad led the church to build a building over the basement. The Lord blessed and the church grew during his ministry there.

While I was finishing high school in Toronto, I began to work with Harold Elder as a song leader, helping to start a new church in Iola, Kansas. We met in an old dilapidated house that had gone through the 1951 flood.

One Sunday while I was there, four students from Baptist Bible College came to a Sunday service. I had them introduce themselves and among them was Jerry Falwell, who later pastored Thomas Road Baptist Church in Lynchburg, Virginia. He also founded Liberty University and was very influential in thousands of people being saved in the 1950s-1990's. Years later, at a fellowship meeting, I asked Bro. Falwell if he remembered that Sunday in the little church in Iola, Kansas and he said that he did.

My favorite cousin, Pheobe, would come play the piano in Iola on occasion. I have so many happy memories there.

When I think back on my early years when I was first called into the ministry, I remember the wonderful friends we made. I don't know that it would have happened without Bro. Rutter praying for us and pushing us to go out and preach on street corners. It took us out of our comfort zone and taught us to "go to the highways and hedges" and preach the gospel. Thank the Lord for Bro. Rutter!

All the pastors that signed our ordination certificate are now in heaven, including my dad. I look forward to being with them soon. Revelation 14:13 says, "And their works do follow them."

Chapter 14

BRO. ART WILSON:
MY SECOND FATHER

I LEFT IOLA AND WENT TO MANHATTAN, Kansas in hopes of starting a church there. While living in Manhattan, I received word from Bro. Art Wilson to please contact him. I had met him at a national fellowship meeting at Wichita Baptist Tabernacle, where he was the pastor. While I was there, I stayed in the home of Bro. Leslie Baker and was surprised to discover that Iola, Kansas was his hometown. Bro. Baker became one of my dearest friends and later became a missionary to Haiti for over thirty years.

When I talked to Bro. Art on the phone, he told me that he was getting ready to hold a meeting in Junction City, Kansas and wanted to know if I would come work with him and his evangelistic team. Most likely, Bro. Burt Rutter, my original pastor, recommended me. He was saved under Bro. Art's ministry and they were close friends.

The next two years were among the greatest years of my life. Bro. Art was such a great man of wisdom and sacrifice, and a friendship developed between us. He treated me like a son: provided me a place to live, food to eat, shoes and clothes as needed. I was not guaranteed a salary, but I was always taken care of. I would help him drive, run errands, lead songs, and help set up for large meetings. We had meetings in Boise, Idaho, Pittsburg, Kansas, and a county-wide meeting in Ogalla, Nebraska. We also attended the dedication of the magnificent new building of Temple Baptist Church in Detroit, Michigan, where Beachum Vick was Pastor. I thank the Lord for his influence in my life.

Hundreds of miles of travel were spent with Bible quizzes and instruction. Bro. Art kept everything exciting. There was never a dull moment. When Bro. Art was in the pulpit, he was always well prepared. He became a second father to me—so unselfish and kind.

Chapter 15

NORMA LUELLA SMITH: SWEPT OFF MY FEET

NORMA LUELLA SMITH WAS A twenty-two-year-old, beautiful girl, with dark brown hair and dark brown eyes. Her personality was pretty quiet but a little feisty. I was eighteen when we met.

She grew up on a farm in Mulvane, Kansas with her parents, Leo and Sylvia Smith. Together they had twelve children and were very poor. Leo Smith was musical and could play any instrument. As the children got older, he taught each of them to play an instrument and sing harmonies. At night, they would sit around the fire and sing. The three oldest sisters, Mary, Norma, and Carrie started a trio and sang at rodeos on weekends. The family harmony was amazing. They even made a record!

The family worked hard every day of the week and going to church was never a thought. Leo's mother, Grandma Smith, loved the Lord and witnessed to her son often. Grandma Smith prayed daily that her son and his family would receive the Lord as their Savior.

At twenty-four and twenty-two, Norma and her older sister, Mary, decided to leave home, get jobs, and live out on their own in Wichita, Kansas. Even though they were in their twenties, their dad wouldn't let them leave home until they had money saved up for at least one month's rent. Norma's brother, Leo, was in the Army at the time and wanted to help his sisters with an apartment, so he sent them $200.

So, Mary and Norma were off to Wichita, Kansas and both got jobs at a bank. A friend from the bank invited them to church. One Sunday morning, they got on the bus to try and find their friend's church, but got lost. So instead, they ended up at the Wichita Baptist Tabernacle, where my second father, Bro. Art Wilson, was the pastor. It was definitely a God thing! They heard the gospel and both were saved. From that point on, they started using their musical talents for the Lord. Later, Carrie would join her sisters and accept the Lord, making the trio complete.

While I was visiting Bro. Art, I noticed Norma singing in the choir. From the start, I felt like we were a perfect match. She was a beautiful young lady with a talented voice and a deep love for the Lord. Norma taught a Sunday school class of fourteen-year-old girls. One of those girls, Phyllis Smith, ended up marrying Bro. Ray Melugine, the pastor who followed Bro. Art Wilson at the Wichita Baptist Tabernacle.

It was such a joyful time. She swept me off my feet!

The next year, we dated between my travels to revival meetings. We would challenge each other to memorize a certain passage from the Bible, and then quote it from memory on our next date. Most of our dates revolved around church activities, like visitations and youth gatherings.

On our early dates, Bro. Art would allow me to use his car, but eventually Norma got a car. We would go to youth activities like hobo stews, where everyone would bring a can of anything they liked, mix it all together, and add it to the pot. Someone brought rattlesnake meat, but no one knew until after we had finished eating!

Bro. Art enjoyed teasing Norma while she was in the choir, so he could see her dark eyes sparkle. *My*! How Norma, Mary, and Carrie could bless hearts with their singing! There is nothing like sister harmony! Thank God that Norma's dad taught all his children to play an instrument and sing. God sure knew that would be an asset in later years, because one day, Norma would play the piano for our church services.

The Lord used the sisters in such a great way. Norma and her sister Mary became instrumental in influencing their younger siblings to become faithful Christians! Three of Norma's brothers, Leo, Loyal, and Allen, became preachers. Her sister Pearl's husband, Bill Bramblett, was a pastor and, of course, Norma married me and became a faithful pastor's wife for many years until her death in 1994.

The Lord knew Norma would be the perfect helpmate for me—the perfect pastor's wife, friend, and mother to our children. We had almost thirty-nine wonderful years together. Thank the Lord for Norma and the blessing she was to everyone that met her. The Lord only knows how many people were saved from Norma Luella Smith Wambsganss' testimony. Truly, a life well lived!!!

Mary, Carrie, and Norma Smith (1953)

Chapter 16

FIRST TIME PASTOR AND HAMBURGER GRAVY

WHEN NORMA AND I MARRIED, I had just accepted a call to pastor the Bible Baptist Church in Eureka, Kansas. I would be the third pastor of the church started by Eugene Chichester. The second pastor was Bro. Sam Herring. One of his sons, Dennis, remained at the church and had a job at a local grocery store. Over the years, he would become a great friend and serve as a missionary.

The church met in an old feed store building. The membership was small and consisted of Bob and Roberta Samuels, the Reynolds family, and three widows. Even though the building was crude, it was all we could afford. For a while, Mrs. Reynolds played the piano for services, but when she could no longer do it, Norma taught herself to play. Her dad had taught her to play the guitar, and she knew the cord structures. She just practiced and practiced until she became a good pianist. She learned a new song each week, and her selection of songs grew and grew.

During this time, the church wasn't financially able to support a pastor, so I worked at the bakery making $17.00/ week take-home pay, while Norma used that time to practice. Our rent was $35.00/ month, and our weekly food budget was $5.00.

Fisher's meat market was across the street from the bakery, and they would run specials on ground meat: 5 lbs. for 85 cents. Being from a family of twelve children, Norma knew how to make a delicious meal from very little. Hamburger gravy over homemade biscuits is still a favorite of mine!

41

Chapter 17

OUR HIVE OF B'S

ALOVING FAMILY IS A WONDERFUL GIFT from God, and one of
the most thrilling times in life is the anticipation of being parents!
We had six children in ten years!

Norma and I were both so thrilled when the doctor told us that she
was pregnant. In those days, ultra-sound was not available, so we had to
wait until the birth to know if the baby was a boy or a girl. As soon as we
found out there was a baby on the way, we began to plan, pray, and dream.
We weren't the only ones excited—this baby would be the first grandchild
on both sides of the family!

Around the same time, we found out Norma's sister, Carrie, was also
going to have a baby. It became a race to see who would be the first to
deliver! We won!

Funny thing, Dr. Francis Basham, the doctor who delivered me, delivered our cute baby girl, Rebecca (Becky) Lynn on, of all days . . . Valentine's
Day, February 14, 1965! To our surprise, a little over an hour away, Norma's
sister, Carrie, had just delivered a baby boy on Valentine's Day too! His
name was Wesley Guthrie. When we compared times, Becky had been
born just minutes before Wesley. Norma's parents had been blessed with
their first grandson and granddaughter on the same day. They have always
declared that they are twin cousins.

Less than two years later, the doctor gave us the great news that our
family was about to grow and we were so excited! As the time came near,
we tried our best to get this baby born. We did things that we thought
would help the baby arrive, but nothing worked. Among the things we
tried was driving for long rides on bumpy roads and running over railroad

42

tracks. One day, we decided to have a picnic lunch in a nearby park. I had forgotten to bring any matches to start the fire, so I rolled up a paper sack and used the car's cigarette lighter to try to get the fire started. And boy did I ever get a fire going! I set the whole park on fire! (Moral of the story: Always make sure you are prepared to start a fire.) But even after all of that, the baby still did not come!

Finally, the night arrived. Delivery pains came and all of us present were saying, "Norma wait, it's just three minutes until your birthday." But as we all know, babies have a mind of their own. We asked the doctor to put March 23 on the birth certificate, since it was just three minutes before, but he refused. So, on March 22, 1958, we welcomed our second baby girl, Bonnie Ruth, and she had a birthday all her own. We were overjoyed!

Less than two years later, while we were living and serving in Prescott, Kansas, we were filled with glee to learn our children would number three! The closest hospital was sixteen miles away in Ft. Scott, Kansas. I had just accepted the call to pastor the church in Dodge City, Kansas, but we didn't want to go until Norma gave birth. But when she arrived, she stole the show! She was born on May 12, 1960.

Our third girl was a charm! We named her Brenda Grace and she proudly took her place. Now we had daughter three and was she ever the life of the party. Brenda fit right into Dodge City, "Cowtown of the West." I'm sure you may have guessed our family is still to be blessed. Then we were told that another sibling was on the way. What a joy, it may be a boy!

As the time drew near, Norma's sister, Mary, came to help us prepare for our fourth arrival, because our younger three daughters took their time to be delivered. On August 9, 1962, this baby was born in a hurry on the cart on the way to the delivery room. I was at work and didn't have time to get to the hospital before the baby came. When I arrived at the hospital, Mary met me, and I asked if it was a boy or a girl, but she would not tell me, she said I had to ask Norma. When I got to the hospital room, Norma was excited to tell me it was a boy!

We named him William David, and I had my boy named after me. How proud I was! I had always wished that if I ever had a boy, I wanted him to be *all boy*. Did I ever get my wish! Soon after he could walk, he was throwing rocks at cars. That was a little more boy than I bargained for! As he grew older, he was on the high school wrestling team and the football team.

Don't hang up now, we had a boy, but it's not over yet.

We had a big surprise on the way and by this time, Norma had perfected childbirth. Her mother had twelve children, and we were well on our way. When we got news of a new one coming, it was as thrilling as the first. We had no idea what was in store. Our new precious bundle arrived on March 8, 1964, and we named her Naomi Beth.

The next day was Sunday and the kids and I stopped at the hospital on our way to TV Altar, our television program. We had no idea that Beth was born a celebrity. Two whole pages of our newspaper, *The Dodge City Daily Globe*, were devoted to her birth. She was the 5,000th baby to be born in Trinity Hospital. There were pictures of Norma and baby Beth, along with a picture of the very first baby born at Trinity hospital and her mother. By then, that first baby was a grown woman. Many city merchants had placed ads in the local paper offering free gifts to us for our celebrity baby, Beth. *My!* Did she ever enter Dodge City with a splash! For me, Beth is still a hero today!

Well, every train has to have a caboose. Once again, we received a precious gift from God: Betty Joanna was born on January 21, 1966. She became the best dressed girl in town with all of her sisters' hand-me-downs. Cry, cry aloud, our whole family was so proud! As Betty grew, she became such a funny little girl. She would be in front of the mirror crying and we would ask her what was the matter? She would reply that she had hurt her own feelings!

She always will be my baby, but it's unbelievable that my baby girl is now a mother of a teenager.

Chapter 18

MY DAD'S CONTINUAL CALL AND SACRIFICE

A S MY FAMILY WAS EXPANDING, my father was having a successful ministry in Emporia, Kansas. But the Lord burdened my father's heart for Independence, Kansas. It was the largest city in the area. Sometimes the call of God requires sacrifice and this move required my dad to work various jobs, like re-capping tires and driving a ready-mix concrete truck, all while pastoring. Even so, a congregation was established and a building purchased during his pastorate.

Among the people saved were the Musgrove family. One of their sons, Carl, and my sister, Evelyn, met and were married. Carl and Evelyn had four boys: Timmy, Tony, Todd, and Terry. Evelyn's wonderful family was very active in the that church for many years, even after my father moved on. Evelyn, Timmy, and Tony are rejoicing together in heaven now.

After several years of ministry there, The Bible Baptist Church of Augusta, Kansas called my dad to be pastor. It was a baby church, but they did have their own building. My father pastored the church and drove a school bus to bring money home to support the family.

It was while my father pastored there that a blessing came our way. Becky Schmidt, whose parents were missionaries to France, came to visit the church. There she met my brother, Leon. A romance ensued, and they were married. After Leon finished his years at Arlington Baptist College, they were approved as missionaries to Spain. While they were there, they were blessed with three boys: Stephen, Andrew, and Phillip. My brother Leon died this year. Thank the Lord for his many years on this earth.

A few years later, the empty nest syndrome settled upon my parents when my younger brother, Paul, was swept off his feet by Marsha Morris. The Morris family was very active in the Augusta church. They married and had two children: Trisha and Aaron. Paul worked in ministry at several churches for a good part of his adult life. He and his son, Aaron, are now in heaven.

Chapter 19

PRAYING AND PLAYING

*Trust in the Lord with all thine heart, lean not unto
thine own understanding. In all thy ways acknowledge
him and he shall direct thy path.*

(PROVERBS 3:5-6)

STARTING NEW CHURCHES WAS always a burden on my dad's heart. When my dad went to pastor Bible Baptist Church in Independence, he became good friends with Dan Baldwin, who was a recent graduate of Baptist Bible College in Springfield, Missouri. Dad's church became the mother church for Dan when he started a new church in Coffeyville, Kansas.

Dan and my dad became real buddies. They preached, prayed, and played together. Starting a new church is always a challenge. There are always great blessings and great burdens; both are part of birthing pains. One day, a real challenge came dad's way.

One evening while we were talking on the phone, my dad was extremely upset. When he got to the church that day, right there was a letter to the pastor which stated, "If you would stop preaching about money and sin, and start preaching the gospel, the Lord would bless more." It was signed, a concerned church member. My dad said, "I know the woman that wrote it." He said that he got down all the Christmas cards and compared the handwriting!

Later on that week, he met with Dan and he asked my dad, "Pastor did you get my note on your pulpit?" What an encourager *he* was! With friends like *that*, who needs enemies? They remained very best friends.

In years to come, Dan became a missionary to Alaska. My father and mother planned a trip to surprise their friend and his family in Rangle, Alaska. They drove to Canada, getting flat tires on very rough roads, they took a ferry to Rangle, Alaska for their surprise visit.

Dan didn't know that they were coming, but by God's grace he was home for the surprise visit! After a short visit, Dan said, "George, I want to show you Alaska!" Dad told him, "That's what I'm here for. I wouldn't have spent the money and driven those rough roads and had the flat tires if I hadn't wanted to see Alaska." Then came the shocker! Dan told my dad that there was only one way to see Alaska: by airplane! Dan had learned how to fly and had an airplane with floats on it to take off from water and land.

You see, my father was deathly afraid of heights and especially flying. When we lived on the farm, my uncle Earnest lived twenty miles north of us. Two of his friends had airplanes and asked my uncle if they could use his pasture for an air strip. He agreed and they built two metal buildings to store their planes in. Occasionally, on a Sunday after church, we would drive the twenty miles north to my Uncle Earnest and Aunt Etta's house and eat Sunday dinner. I wouldn't even wait for dessert but would head out to the pasture where they were flying the planes. I would stand around until I could convince one of the pilots to give me a ride, and they would consent because I was Uncle Earnest's nephew. I would ask my dad if he wanted to go on a plane ride and he would say, "No, not on your life. I'm afraid of those things! I don't trust them!"

If you would've asked him if he believed in airplanes, he would've said, "Of course I do. My brother has an airport. I've seen them crank the motor with the propellers, I've kicked the tires, felt the wings, and I've seen them fly. Of course I believe in airplanes." But if you asked, "Have you ever trusted an airplane, climbed inside, sat down, and fastened the seatbelt?" He would have said no!

He was like so many people who say they believe in God but have never put their total faith and trust in him. It's not enough to believe in God. The Bible tells us in James 2:19-21 that even the devil believes and trembles.

That day in Alaska, my father trusted an airplane with his safety for the first time in his life. With his fist clenched, he said, "If I get back here alive, it's because I trust this airplane and pilot." It was much the same as he did many years ago in a car, outside of the hospital in Eureka, Kansas. He trusted the Lord and said, "I know I'm a sinner and I accept you as my Savior, would you please save me? I'll live for you."

Just like the day he accepted Christ, the trip to Alaska was a life-changer for him. Both were an act of faith, and the Bible says, "Without faith, it is impossible to please God."

After that, the Lord was with him on many airplane flights to the Holy Land, missionary trips, and many flights between Washington and Kansas.

'Tis so sweet to trust in Jesus, just to take him at his word. Just to rest upon his promise. Just to know thus saith the Lord.

Oh, how wonderful it is to walk by faith!

Chapter 20

CAR WRECK WITH BECKY AND BONNIE

THROUGHOUT MY LIFE, I have never had trouble going to sleep. I can lay down flat on the floor and, before you know it, I'm sound asleep. There are even times when I should be awake, but I fall off to sleep. This happened several times while I was driving!

Once, while driving from Augusta back to Dodge City from a fellowship meeting in Wichita, Kansas, falling asleep turned tragic. I had to get back home in time to go to work at 8:00 a.m. I knew I was tired, and rolled down my window. All at once, I saw headlights coming straight toward me. I had my two oldest daughters with me in the pickup truck. They had sung at the fellowship meeting. I swerved, but not in time to avoid a head-on collision. The other car landed out in the wheat field, and our vehicle was off the road in a ditch.

Becky's head was cut, and my leg was badly broken. The three of us crawled out of the windshield. It was dark, but we were able to make it up to the highway. One of the girls said, "Daddy, we didn't pray before we left Augusta." We stopped right there and had a prayer meeting in the middle of the highway. Because of the darkness, I couldn't see the other car and didn't know if they were dead or alive. We soon heard someone yell, "Are you alright? We are fine, we all had our seatbelts on." We were driving a late model truck that belonged to my boss, Gerald Bailes.

Soon, a highway patrolman and an ambulance arrived. I received a ticket and my dad was called. He ended up paying the ticket. A day or two later, I was discharged from the Pratt, Kansas Hospital with a cast all the way up to my hip. I remember Norma saying that helping me around and attending to our six children was one of the hardest times of her life.

As soon as I could, I went to the salvage yard and told Mr. Bailes how sorry I was for wrecking his truck, and that I wanted him to deduct what I owed him from my paycheck each week, until it was paid for. He said, "Bill, I had liability on the truck, so the other car will be paid for and don't worry about the truck." What a great friend indeed!

George and Eleanor Wambsganss Family Around 1951

Bro. Bill Wambsganss (1953)

1960s-1970s

Chapter 21

MY CALL TO DODGE CITY, KANSAS

*Without faith, it's impossible to please God. And, without a
doubt, our greatest blessings are when we step out by faith.*

—BRO. BILL

S UCH WAS THE CASE IN 1960 when Bro. Ray Wilson, Art Wilson's
son, asked me to come to Dodge City, Kansas and hold a revival
meeting for the Bible Baptist Church. Bro. Ray Wilson was single and
worked as a cook in a café for a living. The church he had established
eighteen months before was a struggling, baby church. I accepted his
invitation and held the revival in the dead of winter. As I remember it,
we had seven in attendance the first Sunday meeting; the second Sunday
we had fourteen.

As I pastored the Prescott Baptist Church in Prescott, Kansas, the
Lord had blessed our family. The church congregation was seventy-five
years old and had a church parsonage across the street. Like the Apostle
Paul, I was still bi-vocational and felt satisfied and secure. I worked as the
parts manager at Kippers Chevrolet in Pleasanton, Kansas, eight miles
from Prescott. The Lord had certainly blessed me with a wonderful family,
a loving wife, two precious daughters, and another on the way. What more
could a man want?

Then the shocker came: Bro. Ray Wilson called me and said that he
had resigned as pastor of the church in Dodge City, Kansas. I hadn't even
known that he was considering leaving the church. Then he said, "The
church voted to call you as pastor."

Would I go or would I not go? I had to pray, "God, what is your will?" If I accepted it, I would get the same salary Bro. Ray got, which was nothing, and I knew I would have to get a new job. Even though there had been one church giving us support for a while, in those days, raising support to start a church was not the norm. After prayer, I felt it was God's plan for us to move to Dodge City and continue the work Bro. Ray Wilson had started.

What a challenge to step out and trust God's hand to lead us! A pastor friend in Butler, Missouri loaned me his enclosed trailer to pull behind my Oldsmobile, packed with everything we owned.

Our third baby girl, Brenda Grace, was born on May 12 in Prescott, Kansas and, soon after, we moved about 300 miles away to Dodge City. I was twenty-four years old, and this was one of the biggest steps of faith in my lifetime.

Amazingly, the small congregation had put together enough money to rent us an upstairs apartment at 802 W. Oak. Our landlord lived in the ground floor beneath us. As soon as we moved in, I went to Frank Epp Chevrolet and was hired on in the parts department at $40.00 a week. Eddie Mahieu was a fellow worker I met there. He is now eighty-six years old and still a good friend today.

Our church was a cement block building located in the south part of town and had previously been a blacksmith shop. It was a very crude building indeed, but it was all the church could afford. Our congregation was three young married couples and a middle-aged family, all of which were of meager means.

Before I came, the congregation had stepped out in faith to buy the building. They had also accumulated some debt from a tent revival and were three months behind on payments for the building, having accumulated $1,500 of unpaid debt. But none of this was too big for God! He knew the needs, and we were confident that he would provide—we just didn't know how . . .

One Sunday morning we had a visitor to our church service, Jim Childress, the service manager at Frank Epp Chevrolet. I had made friends with Jim at work and found out he was a former pastor in Tennessee. Jim enjoyed the service and invited three sisters to visit with him the next Sunday. The sisters, who had never been married and lived together, shared that they had prayed for years for a church with sound doctrine to be established in Dodge City. They joined the church and were such an encouragement to a young pastor.

Early one morning in the middle of the week, I heard a knock on our apartment door. The youngest of those three sisters was standing there and said, "Bro. Wambsganss, here is a check for your church and also here is a check from my sister. The Lord laid it on our hearts to give them." I was shocked when I saw the amount of $1,000 on each check. The next day, early in the morning, another knock came to my door. There stood the same lady, and she said, "My other sister said she felt the Lord wanted her to give $1,000 too," and we had a total of $3,000! In 1960, that was a lot of money. By today's calculation, that would equal $15,000.

What a blessing at a time when the Church needed it so much! God's timing is always right! Thank the Lord for teaching me this lesson!

Chapter 22

THE SINGING B'S AND HONEY TOO

DURING MY EARLY YEARS, it was my privilege to meet many pastors and missionaries and to become friends with their children. Many of their kids loved the ministry and grew up to become preachers and missionaries themselves. Occasionally, I would meet those who were not happy being a preacher or missionaries' child. Norma and I discussed this problem and hoped that the children God gave us would love the Lord, love us, and the ministry.

We decided we would have a few guidelines that we would follow. First, we would never disagree in front of the children about discipline or really anything else. We might discuss it in private, but the kids would never know. Second, we would show love and respect for each other, both in public and in private. Third, we would not complain about lack of finances, but just trust the Lord. Finally, we would never discuss church members' problems and struggles with our children or in front of them.

We were so blessed to pastor four churches. We loved every member and we felt they really loved us. Thank God our six children love the Lord. We are all human and have our weaknesses, but God has been faithful!

We purposefully named our children with Biblical names, either their first name or middle name. But we also have shortened some so that we all start with B's. I'm Bro. Bill. Then there's Becky, Bonnie, Brenda, Billy, Beth and Betty Jo. Norma didn't start with a "B," so we called ourselves, *The Singing B's and Honey Too!*

As a family, it has been thrilling to be used in ministry and be able to travel to many states to preach and sing. Every time a baby was born, it was

60

a thrill to have a new voice join our musical family. Soon after singing in a church, we would head out to the closest Dairy Queen to celebrate! If I had been given the privilege of planning the itinerary for our family, I couldn't have done a better job than what the Lord has done.

Norma was the musician, and she worked hours upon hours with the kids to help them learn parts, lyrics, etc. It wasn't just *my* ministry—it was *our* ministry! Norma and I only sang a couple of songs together. One was *Where Jesus is 'tis Heaven There*, and *What a Day That Will Be*.

I would attribute the closeness of our family to God's grace and the hours we spent together working toward a common purpose, serving the Lord together through preaching, singing, and music that brought glory to God. Each child had a part to sing, and that created great harmony in music, as well as in our family.

Norma, our honey, is already with the Lord. I can imagine her singing in the heavenly choir and soon I will be joining her. *What a Day That Will Be!*

Chapter 23

OUR RADIO AND TELEVISION MINISTRY

WE BEGAN A TV MINISTRY IN 1963, but it started out as a radio program. It's amazing to see how God worked! Having worked for Bro. Art Wilson and knowing that my father had also used radio as an outreach, I contacted a new radio station in Dodge City. They told me a fifteen-minute program on Sunday mornings would cost $14.00 per week. So, I began preaching each Sunday on the radio.

Now, channel 6 was a rural TV station located twenty-five miles west of Dodge City. A man who attended our church worked at the Phillips 66 gas station and told me that the gas station had recently bought TV advertising on Channel 6. He mentioned our radio program to the salesman. The salesman said, "Tell your pastor I will sell him TV time for just what he's paying for radio." He said that a program from a church in Cimarron, Kansas was discontinuing and that I should call him.

When I heard about the offer from the salesman, I felt like it was too good to be true! To my surprise, a few days later, the salesman showed up at the salvage yard, where I was currently working. He told me that if I would sign a year contract, he would sell me a fifteen-minute program on Sunday mornings at 8:00 a.m. for $11.00 per week.

A few hours later, the station manager, Wendell Elliott, called to tell me that he didn't know what had gotten into the salesman, but that $11.00 a week was way too low and that he would change the contract to $11.00 a week for six months, but raise the price to $14.00 for the rest of the year. So, of course I agreed, and we had a deal! (After all, we were currently paying $14.00 for a fifteen-minute radio program that had been discontinued.)

In those days, there was no cable TV and people had to use antennas on the tops of their houses. We would leave Dodge City at 7 a.m. and drive the twenty-five miles to the station for our fifteen-minute live program we called *TV Altar*. There was no pre-taping available then. Bro. Richard Buchanan, our church song leader, would MC the first part and also run the camera. Mrs. Humble, our church organist, would sing a special while Norma played the piano, and I would preach. The only staff from the TV station present was the engineer.

Norma had been working with Becky and Bonnie, who began singing regularly on *TV Altar*. Becky was seven years old and Bonnie was five. Janice Stone, a church member with a beautiful voice, started singing on *TV Altar* also. A few years later, Brenda joined in singing the low alto part with Becky and Bonnie. My son, Bill, ran the camera when he became a teenager. After several more years, Beth and Betty Jo also joined in singing. Getting all six kids up at 6 a.m. to be ready to leave the house by 7 a.m., then drive to the TV station and be able to sing with good voices was a chore! But our children's best memories are surrounded by those times.

We would get many letters from people who lived in rural areas and they encouraged our hearts. We developed lifelong friendships with people who watched and visited us, by driving a long distance a couple times a year.

Several years passed and the station upgraded to 100,000 watts and became full color. Another gospel program after our fifteen-minute program cancelled their spot, and the station had to fill in with other programs. I called and asked if we could have the extra fifteen minutes to give us a thirty-minute program. The station manager agreed, and I was excited about the new possibilities.

The TV program spanned nineteen years while I was Pastor in Dodge City and continued on after I accepted the call to pastor Westside Baptist Church in Bremerton, Washington. Precious memories!

Chapter 24

ONE OF MY FAVORITE MEMORIES: BOB MORRIS

BOB MORRIS WAS A PREACHER friend of mine who pastored the First Baptist Church in Great Bend, Kansas. He would come over so we could go soul winning together. One evening, we visited a man who owned two businesses in Dodge City. After visiting and witnessing to him, he prayed and asked the Lord to forgive him of his sins. After which he went to a cabinet and took out his bottles of liquor and poured them out in his sink. He then said, "Bro. Bill, stay for a while. I want to make a telephone call." The call was to his grandfather in Arkansas. He said to him, "Grandpa, I just got saved and I want you to talk to the preacher." Evidently, his grandpa had prayed for him for years!

Bro. Morris would be so excited about someone getting saved, that he would have trouble calming down. We would go to a truck stop, drink coffee, and sit, thanking the Lord for his goodness and enjoy a time of rejoicing about the life that God changed!

Chapter 25

DON SMITH: A LIFE CHANGED FROM TRAGEDY

AN EVENT HAPPENED THAT would change the Dodge City church forever. One Saturday, while working at the salvage yard just before Labor Day weekend, we were getting ready to go home when I heard a scream and looked up on the hill. The huge yard truck was rolling down the hill by itself. I saw a body lying on the ground. It was a co-worker and friend that I had been witnessing to. I ran up the hill so I could pray with him, but when I got there, although his eyes were open and he appeared to be looking at me, I realized it was just his body. He was already gone.

He'd been riding on the side of the truck, his foot had slipped and he'd fallen under the huge wheels. I looked up to the top of the hill and there were two men kneeling. One was the driver of the truck, and the other was an unsaved mechanic named Don Smith. The driver was screaming over and over, "Oh God! I killed a man!" Don was telling him, "All we can do is pray."

Later that evening, I went to the driver's home and he made a profession of faith in Jesus. I was asked to preach at the funeral. I'll never forget the grief that his Godly parents and the grieving co-workers showed that day.

A few weeks later, Don Smith brought his family to church. He came forward at the end of the service and trusted Jesus as his savior. His life drastically changed. Soon after, his mother, father, two sisters, and brother-in-law trusted Jesus too. Many of Don's friends came to know the Lord because of his testimony. It's so good to know that many of his family are still serving the Lord and some in full-time ministry.

About two years after his salvation, Don became the youth minister of our church in Dodge City. The youth department was the largest we had ever had while I was pastor there. During the time he served as youth pastor, our youth took a mission trip to help a baby church in Queens, a burrow of New York City. We held a revival and then Bible school in the park. That was in 1976 and it was a joy for our teens to be able to sing the song *Statue of Liberty* for the 200-year celebration of our great nation. It was amazing.

After many years of faithful service in the church in Dodge City, Don felt the call of God to go work with the Ute Indians in Colorado. He and his sweet wife, Phyllis, served in the Four Corners area. They started three Native American churches and had extensive tent revivals. Living in a very small travel trailer, they had just enough support from churches to survive. They both couldn't be happier having served the Lord together for over thirty years. They have many rewards in heaven.

Looking back in the rearview mirror of my life, I have come to understand that God was at work in and through my life as much when I was working a secular job as He was when I was pastoring full time. Thank the Lord for his plan!

Chapter 26

THE BIG FLOOD

There are many times in the life of a church, as well as in the lives of Christians, that God allows storms to come, but they always end with a rainbow and precious promises from God.

—BRO. BILL

SUCH WAS THE CASE IN 1965 . . . we heard on the news that there had been heavy rains and flooding in Eastern Colorado, and that a giant wall of water was coming our way. It was moving slowly, but it was very big. As we heard the flood was approaching, the whole city took thousands of sandbags and placed them along the banks of the river and buildings close by. Normally in Dodge City, the river was just a few feet across.

In 1951, there had been a huge flood on the river, and many believed that this one wouldn't be any bigger than that one had been. It took about a week for the floodwaters to make their way to Dodge City. One minute, the river was not much wider than you could jump across, but within an hour it was two miles wide. Far greater than the 1951 flood.

In our church building, we had moved the piano, all my books from my office, and other important items to a raised platform the week prior to the flood. We were told the 1951 flood had not made it to our building, so we didn't think we had anything to worry about. Even so, we went ahead and put hundreds of sandbags around the building, just to be sure.

After the floodwaters subsided, we were allowed access to our church building and discovered it had been much worse than we originally thought. We found that the mud from the flood was three to four feet deep in the building, and all the contents that we thought were safe had been ruined. All of south Dodge City was a disaster zone.

I don't even know if flood insurance was available back then, but we didn't have any. We began the process of trying to clean out the building. The mud we shoveled would run right back in, so we were forced to wait until the mud receded outside in order to clean the building inside. The aroma of the mud was worse than the smell of the feed yards and will never be forgotten! We were never able to conduct services in that building again. Hundreds of people were suffering similar losses to ours. But it's through trying times like this that you know God is walking with you.

Retus and Helene Humble were faithful members of the church who lived in a beautiful home on high ground in north Dodge City and graciously offered their basement as a meeting place for church services. After some time, we were able to rent Northwest Elementary School to conduct services, but continued looking for a piece of land to build a building.

Bro. Perryman, a pastor in Overland Park, Kansas, offered us their blueprints from the church building they had just built. He said it cost them $35,000 to build a beautiful, new building. At the same time, The Church of Christ had just built a new building in far north Dodge City. Their old building was in a great location and still a very nice building. It was completely furnished, had a baptistery, and would have cost over $100,000 to build. The building was sitting empty.

We scheduled a meeting with our men and the men from their church. Another church in town, Central Christian, had offered to buy it for $50,000, but it fell through. The Church of Christ offered to sell it to us for the same amount of money. I told them about the church in Kansas City and told them we could give them $35,000 for their building, but if they couldn't take that we would understand, but would build a new building. They said they would present it to their church for a vote and let us know.

In a few days, they contacted us and said they would accept our offer and, surprisingly, said they would give us a year to raise the money. We went to a savings and loan and borrowed $30,000 and then sold $5,000 in church bonds. The savings and loan requested that we offer a guarantee backup letter from our church headquarters. Since we were Independent Baptists and not a part of an association, I contacted Bro. Art Wilson and he sent us a letter from his church aid association. That was fine with them.

Soon we were in our new church home—miracle of miracles! God gave us a beautiful church building, and we were as excited as a child with a new toy! At the time of the flood, we would have never dreamed of the wonderful blessing that was waiting for us.

Sixty plus years later, the building is still being used to spread the gospel message that Jesus saves! It was so good to see so many familiar faces at the 60th Anniversary of the church in Dodge City, and to remember scores of others that served there, but who are now with the Lord. The Bible Baptist Church of Dodge City, Kansas is now pastored by Bro. Shrock. God's work there still goes on. Thank the Lord!

> *Some through the waters, some through the flood,*
> *some through the fire, but all through the blood.*
> *Some through great sorrow, but God gives a song.*
> *In the night season and all the day long.*

Chapter 27

GO WEST YOUNG MAN

THERE'S AN OLD SAYING FROM colonial days that goes, "Go west young man, go west." Little did I know that the stories my great-grand-father told me would come alive in my own lifetime when I was called to pastor the Bible Baptist Church in Dodge City, Kansas.

Television was in its early days and for seventeen years the TV program that dominated the airwaves was Gunsmoke, depicting Matt Dillon, Wyatt Earp, Doc, Festus and Miss Kitty. Dodge City, Kansas became the number one tourist attraction in the state. A local radio station adopted a slogan saying, "Dodge City's future lies in its past." Among the most popular places was the Longbranch Saloon.

In the 1880's, the cattle drive that originated in Texas kept Dodge City thriving. It was there that the Santa Fe Railroad from the eastern states ended, and the cattle were loaded on a train and sent to markets. The cowboys, who had not seen civilization for many weeks, came to the end of the trail here and celebrated. It seemed like anything went . . . drinking, fighting, and sometimes even death after a gunfight. Sin was the norm!

But there was some testimony of Jesus present. At the museum at Boot Hill, I saw an old, portable pump organ that was said to be used by a street preacher. In the early 1900s, the famous preacher, Billy Sunday, held a revival and a medical doctor was saved. Fifty years later, while I was pastoring in Dodge City, there were people who still made fun of his old-time-hellfire preaching.

When preacher friends and guests would visit us, I delighted in taking them to the old front street replica to see the steam engine train. It was fun to see how nervous they would get as we entered the Longbranch

Saloon, where the favorite drink was a sarsaparilla (root beer). Then we would climb up to Boot Hill, visit the replica of the old cemetery, and read the tombstones. One read, "He ran for Sheriff in 1864 and ran from the Sheriff in 1869." We could look over to the right and see the hangman's noose hanging from a tree, but before we left Boot Hill, we had to visit the authentic Ft. Dodge jail, built of logs and just a few feet square. It had been moved in one piece to Boot Hill. It had bars on the windows, a heavy wooden door, a wooden floor, and a bar on the outside to secure it closed. I enjoyed showing it off!

A few days ago, I was talking to the evangelist Bob Smith, and he told me that he still remembers me getting him to go in the jail, locking the door, leaving him inside, and walking away. Being as kind as I am, I did go back and let him out! Believe it or not, he's still my friend today!

In the years before I arrived in Dodge City, preacher friends of mine, Clifford Clark and Al Wells, had gospel radio programs there. Art Wilson held a tent revival too. By 1960, it was no more evil than any average city of its size. Throughout the city were those who loved the Lord, and it was a great place to live. Two of the largest cattle auctions in the United States were located there, along with many large feed lots and processing plants. The city numbered close to 20,000 and was made up of down home, hard-working, family people. It was surprising to see policemen on horseback. I thought our 300-acre farm back in eastern Kansas was large, but out here in western Kansas, a big farm was thousands of acres.

In the years to come, I was asked to officiate at the funeral of the lady who owned the second largest cattle auction. She had accepted Christ as her Savior many years before, under the ministry of Al Wells in Lakin, Kansas.

It was a time of my most precious memories. What a place to live! God knew what he was doing. May the Lord be praised!

But this is not the end . . . great days are still ahead!!!

Chapter 28

BLOOM YOUTH CAMP

IT'S SO WONDERFUL TO BE ABLE to feel the unseen hand of the Lord working behind the scenes of our lives and ministry. One day, I got a call from a listener of *TV Altar* who said he watched the program every Sunday from Bloom, Kansas, which was twenty-five miles southeast of Dodge City. He asked if we would come down on a Sunday afternoon and hold services in their nice school building and gymnasium. The school had consolidated with the Minneola, Kansas school and the Bloom school was not being used on a regular basis. We were thrilled to go each Sunday afternoon. God blessed and souls were saved. I remember one man who shook like a leaf when he came forward at the invitation to accept the Lord as his Savior.

One day, the man who invited us to hold services there asked, "Bro. Bill, could you use this building for the Lord's service?" The building included 4.5 acres, a lighted ball field, a beautiful gymnasium, and a commercial kitchen and cafeteria. The man was a member of the Bloom Township Board and led them in a township election. They voted to sell us the property for a very good price. It was such a blessing.

We used the property to hold a Bible Institute, youth center, retreats, and youth camps. Many souls were saved and lives were transformed. After many years, hail and windstorms made it impossible to maintain the insurance and to keep the building in good condition. But for many years, God allowed us to see Him working in so many lives through that building. To God be the glory!

Chapter 29

BRO. BAKER: CALLED TO SERVE IN HAITI AND BILLY LOSES SOME WEIGHT

BRO. GEORGE LESLIE BAKER was one of our hard working members in the church in Dodge City. He had just gone through a tragic divorce, and I took him with me to a missions conference at Tulsa Baptist Temple where Clifford Cliff was pastor. Our daughters were asked to provide special music for the conference.

Eighty-five-year-old Granny Holderman was a widow who was greatly used of God in Haiti, the poorest country in the western hemisphere. She was a medical doctor's widow and went to the mission field after her husband's death. Bro. Baker's heart was broken and he told the Lord, "If you could use an old widow lady in Haiti, maybe you could use me there too." A few evenings later, he had a life changing dream in which he saw multitudes of people marching off a cliff into the raging flames of hell. The closer he got, he could see that they were dark faces and, in his heart, he knew they were Haitians.

Could God use him? He certainly did! He lived there in severe poverty for over thirty-five years. He was 50+ years when he began serving in Haiti. He lived just like they lived, on very meager means. Conditions were so bad, that the average American would never even consider it. A loaf of their native homemade bread, a jar of peanut butter, and a couple dozen eggs would sustain him. The natural water contained amoebas and could make you really sick, so he tried to stay away from it, but sometimes he couldn't.

My most frequent trips out of the United States were to Haiti in order to hold camps for my good friend. It was my privilege to go visit him four times and on one of my trips, I took my son, Billy when he was about twelve years old. He enjoyed the sites and became a close friend with a Haitian boy about his same age. The crude building where we met for youth camp was so dilapidated that you could look out through the walls of sticks and mud and see them bring up baby goats and butcher them out in the open where everyone could see. The Haitian people were used to that, but not Billy! They would take a machete and chop the meat up, put it in a big cast iron pot, and then bring up water from the river and add it to the pot. This was the same water where they washed themselves, their clothes, and from which the animals drank. They would then add beans or corn and any other veggies they might have on hand. Under the pot, they had homemade charcoal and sticks of wood for the fire to heat the pot. After it had cooked awhile, the Haitian women, who were preparing it, would reach their hands in the pot and pull out a handful to taste it. They would do this until it was done.

Billy could not stomach the food and lost over ten pounds on the trip. Close by, there was a little village with a little market, and Billy went and bought some Haitian made soda pop. The flavors were very different. One was raisin. For those few days, I don't know that he ate anything else. Then the day came when we would return to civilization as we knew it. It was many miles of paths, rough roads, trees, and brush. Finally, we came to a place that resembled a café. We all couldn't wait to get a home cooked meal. We were determined to get fish and chips. But when the meal came, the fish on the plate still had its head attached and it was looking right at us. Billy suddenly lost his appetite! He did eat some of the chips.

When we finally made it to Port-au-Prince, we found a Kentucky Fried Chicken and Billy got some food he would eat. I looked across the room and couldn't believe my eyes. There sat an old friend, John Bailes, from Dodge City, Kansas. He was down there with his airplane, flying missionaries from the Christian Church in Dodge City. His family were close friends. I had worked for his dad, Gerald Bailes, when the church in Dodge City was small. His dad was one of my closest friends.

When we finally made it back to the USA, Billy kissed the ground! Funny thing is, I could never talk him in to going to Haiti with me again. As I look back on it, no one ever went to Haiti with me more than one time . . .

Chapter 30

TRAVELING TO
EUROPE IN 1968

EARLY IN THE YEAR OF 1968, an opportunity of a lifetime came my way: my parents planned a trip to Europe and invited me and my little brother, Paul, along to visit my other brother, Leon, in Spain! Leon had moved to Spain as a missionary with his wife Becky and their boys! Mr. Bailes, my boss, gave me time off work and a good donation for the trip, while Norma graciously agreed to stay home and care for the family.

On the plane, before we crossed the ocean, we looked out the window and saw dozens of little baby chicks running all over the tarmac. They were being flown overseas and one of the boxes had broken open and airline workers were all running around trying to catch them. But we were soon on our way, headed for sights we had never seen before and for memories that would last a lifetime!

When we finally arrived at the Madrid airport, we were greeted by Leon and his family! Bro. Lonnie King and his wife were missionaries to the Canary Islands and offered to transport our group all over Europe in their Volkswagen van.

Among the sights we saw in Madrid were magnificent cathedrals and art galleries. The visit to the Spanish Royal Palace, which had 2,800 rooms with all kinds of gorgeous furnishings, was stunning. The bullfights were attended by thousands. (The Matadors really have the advantage because the bull is always the one that dies while the crowd goes wild, throwing and waving handkerchiefs in the air.) But on our way to the bullfights, we also passed many disabled beggars.

Outside the big city, we saw villages that were hundreds of years old. It seemed that every town had their own large church, mostly Catholic, with a bell tower that was used to call people to worship, give important announcements, or emergencies. When my brother, Paul, saw the big rope hanging down from the bell, he just had to pull it. Leon quickly came to the rescue for fear the whole village would be alerted . . . and it was!

While we were in one of those villages, a sight caught my father's attention that revealed his farmer side. There was an old-time, horse drawn, mowing machine like we had had on the farm. This one was different. The farmer was working a cow and a horse side by side. My father wanted a picture with him driving this unequally yoked team.

We also visited Burgos, Spain, the place where Leon had a church. It was thrilling to see how well he had learned the language. He was naturally conversational and spent a lot of time witnessing to people on the streets there.

We met a pastor in Barcelona, whose wife had died. He had a fourteen-year-old daughter that he became totally responsible for, fulfilling the role of father and mother, so that the church could continue.

In Barcelona, we also visited the place Columbus had sailed from, where there was a tall monument of Columbus pointing to India—where he thought he was headed. Beside the monument was a replica of his boat, *The Santa Maria*.

Leon's wife, Becky, was raised in France as a missionary kid. So, when we traveled to France, Becky did the ordering at a café. You should have seen what they served! But that wasn't all . . . here came course number two. How did they know we were so hungry? Would you believe it? The third time was a charm. Well, we thought we should see if we could eat more, because mother had always told us to clean our plates! Just when we were thinking that it was time to get back on the road because we had a long way to go, here came the main course! I never thought I would see my family have too much food; we were always known for having great appetites.

During our trip, the French President, Charles de Gaulle, was going through a turbulent time: demonstrations, strikes, shutdowns. We hadn't known about the condition and the unrest there. Railroads had not run in so many days that their tracks had begun to rust. There was no gasoline available to the public, and things were pretty much in chaos. After our meal that evening, we were back on the road traveling the many miles to Paris, where we planned to spend the night. We weren't too far down the road when huge army trucks started passing us, headed toward Paris.

The streets of Paris are like the spokes of a big wheel, all running into a hub called The Arch of Triumph, built in memory of Napoleon's great victories in times past. The police were on strike and because all other modes of transportation were closed down, most people were traveling the streets in their cars. The streets became jammed like a huge parking lot. People were yelling, horns and sirens were going off, and lots of people were abandoning their vehicles. We were stuck in the whole mess.

In addition to this, there were youth groups of communist demonstrators handing out leaflets and yelling out slogans. My little brother, Paul, just a teenager and being a patriot, yelled out, "Stupid communists!" My father yelled to Paul, "Be quiet! You will get us all killed!" After hours of impatience and prayer, Leon was able to get the van maneuvered to a side alley at the edge of town, where we found a hotel for the night.

The next day was better. We were able to enjoy the Eiffel Tower and visit the elegant tomb of Napoleon: a rather large, beautiful building with marble, surrounded by his generals. We bought delicious looking pastries from a street vendor and were very surprised when they weren't nearly as sweet as we were used to in the U.S. That evening, we ate at the U.S. Embassy!

Leaving Paris, we also saw the places where Christians had been persecuted and killed during the sixteenth and seventeenth centuries. Of the many sites that we saw as we traveled, one that stood out was a monument in honor of a drummer boy. A large, enemy army was invading the area, and the local people had very little defense, when a lad grabbed his drum and ran to the valley and began to play as loud as he could. The sound echoed back and forth, sounding like a huge army was approaching and the opposing enemy fled in fear.

As we traveled along the highways, we were impressed with the beautiful flowers (I'm sure they must have been planted and cared for). I would frequently see pastor hotels and, me with my brilliant young mind, had it all figured out. Since it was a Catholic country, I asked our missionary chauffeur, Lonnie, if the priests owned the hotels. He told me that the word "pastor" means shepherd. They are places of safety.

While traveling in Germany, we saw many lingering signs of damage from World War II. I was surprised when my brother Leon told me that every town we went through had their own identity as a Catholic village or an Evangelical (Lutheran) one.

When we would stop and shop, I would find a phonebook to try and find the name, Wambsganss. I did not have any success until I got to the Black Forest area. I found it unusual that they listed the occupations of the people listed in their phonebooks.

While we were in Heidelbraun, Germany, we attended church on a Sunday morning with a missionary, Bro. Butcher. Sunday evening, I was privileged to preach in a U.S. military church in Lonstool, Germany. Afterwards, we were invited to the pastor's home and those soldiers got out their guitars and sang. It was such a blessing. That's when I first fell in love with a military church, not knowing God would lead me to pastor one in years to come.

Our next country was Holland. So many things to see: Dutch windmills, wooden shoes, grass roofs on houses, fields of beautiful tulips, as well as a magnificent park that displayed the whole country of Holland in miniature. While there, we were told that Kennedy had been shot—we thought, "That was five years ago . . . news sure moves slow here!" But as the conversation continued, we found out it was *Robert* Kennedy.

The scenes in Switzerland were breathtaking! One of the highlights of our trip was to see the beautiful Alps and visit a Swiss watch factory owned by a Christian man who was a friend of Leon. I bought Norma a watch there. Then we moved on to Italy, where we spent the night in Milan and saw the leaning tower of Pisa. We wanted to have pizza but couldn't find any anywhere! We drove through tunnels on the water and noticed that the cities were filled with graffiti on the walls reading, *YANKEES GO HOME!* Well, I guess we were about ready to go home . . . but before we left, we also visited Austria and Monaco!

Precious memories. How they linger.

Chapter 31

MY DAD'S CALL TO BREMERTON, WASHINGTON

THE LORD REALLY BLESSED my dad's church in Augusta, Kansas. A new parsonage was built and many souls were saved. Among them were two men who moved to Bremerton, Washington to work in the shipyard there. One of these men was Don Williams.

Don started calling my dad and told him that they had started attending a little church called Westside Church in Bremerton. It was two and a half years old, and the pastor's name was Charlie Kearns. His wife had just passed away and he had several children. He resigned not long after his wife's death.

Don told my dad that they desperately needed a pastor and he wanted to know if my dad could help them find one. He repeatedly called my dad and asked him if he had found anyone yet. My father would tell him he had talked to several preachers but hadn't had any luck. Mr. Williams wouldn't give up. My dad finally said he would come preach a revival to hopefully encourage the church, and my parents bought a ticket on a Greyhound bus to the Seattle, Washington area.

My dad said, "As the bus drove down the hill and around the bay, we saw the many Navy ships docked in the Bremerton Naval Shipyard. The Lord immediately broke our hearts."

The congregation numbered between twenty to thirty-some people. The two-room building had, at one time, been a little store building with one room upstairs and one room downstairs. The Lord certainly had to have burdened their hearts to leave a thriving church, new parsonage, children, and grandchildren. Not to mention, Kansas having been the only state they had ever lived in.

It was the best and most fruitful years of my dad's ministry, so the hand of the Lord was definitely in it! It's so amazing how the hand of the Lord was upon him through every move he made in the ministry. My dad never worked at a secular job again, and he hit the road running. He was working harder than he'd ever worked in his life, going door-to-door, witnessing for the Lord, and inviting people to church.

Each Sunday, dad picked up children from two families with his truck with the camper on the back! Driving nineteen miles one way each Sunday was an important part of the Westside Baptist Church growth. The bus ministry was very fruitful and as it grew, became a heartbeat of the church.

One of the girls that my dad picked up, Cindy Coble, grew up in the church and is now a pastor's wife. She married Corey Higdon, a Navy man who was saved during my father's ministry. Corey is now the pastor of the New Testament Baptist Church in Brewster, Washington and is doing a great work there. It's such a blessing to see the fruit that remains.

The first two years, there was some attendance growth, but it was slow. My father would also contact churches in Kansas and Missouri, asking them to give money to purchase property for a permanent home for the church. Throughout the years, my father was a very good businessman, and he was able to purchase five acres on the west side of Bremerton for $12,000.

Soon after the purchase of the property, he got word that a funeral home in downtown Bremerton was selling their land and had a building to get rid of. It was several miles away from the five acres the church had purchased, so dad talked to the owner and was able to persuade him to give the building to the church. Then, my father contacted a moving company that moved large buildings. They agreed to move the building to the new location for $26,000, and he borrowed the money from a bank in Port Orchard.

The building was so large that they had to saw it in half with chainsaws. It was such a spectacular sight that the Bremerton Sun Newspaper covered the move and published large pictures. Free publicity! It would have been financially impossible to purchase that kind of publicity even if they had the money . . . but don't stop now, wait until you hear the rest of the story!

The building was so heavy that the wheels under the structure broke through the street into a storm drain. The next day the newspaper published pictures and a follow-up story. God's unseen hand was definitely at work! Even though the new church property was at the top of a steep hill, the move was completed safely.

Church attendance began to grow! The original members were so faithful, and several navy men accepted Christ as their Savior—navy families were reached! While still in the building, several years later, they were able to burn the mortgage on the loan and have an all-time record attendance of 512!

Chapter 32

A Trip to the Holy Land with Norma

THE GREATEST TRIPS I'VE BEEN on were trips to the Holy Land. My brother Paul worked on staff in Jackson, Michigan with Pastor Berry, who would host a trip to the Holy Land each year. My mother and father went one year and enjoyed it so much, that they offered to pay my way the next year. I jumped at the opportunity and paid Norma's way so she could go along. She was a little reluctant because she wasn't a fan of flying, but later on said it was the best trip of her life. Two other ladies from Bremerton church, Gayle Brown and Mrs. Starbuck, and a teenage girl, Debbie Samley, also went with us.

We landed in Jordan and crossed over the Alanbe Bridge into Israel. The tension was high with machine guns on the sides of the hills and very tight security. They had officers going through the bus checking everybody's passports, but Norma couldn't find hers. She looked everywhere and everyone looked all over the bus. They would not move, but eventually they found it by the bus driver.

Everywhere we went was so exciting, knowing this was where Jesus walked. We went to Bethlehem, where Jesus was born, and I wrote notes to people back home from there. We saw dozens of wonderful sites, such as the Temple Mount, Golgotha, the Garden Tomb (thank God it's empty!), the Garden of Gethsemane, Mount of Olives, and the Sea of Galilee. We also took a side trip to the Rock City of Petra, where Norma and I both rode horses down into in the city, which was a thrill for her since she had been raised riding horses.

We also went swimming in the Dead Sea—so much salt in it, you can't even sink; you float! We flew to Ephesus, where the Apostle Paul spent two years of his ministry. They warned us not to eat the salads because it could make you sick, but Norma ate all her salads and never had a problem.

Another thrill of the trip was taking a boat ride on the Sea of Galilee where we were fed St. Peter's fish. We also saw the place of the feeding of the five thousand and so many other sights: the house where Peter lived and his mother-in-law was healed, the mountain where Elijah called fire down from heaven, and the tomb where Lazarus was raised from the dead. The food, friendship, and scriptural sights sure made the Bible come alive in our minds. It was a trip I will never forget.

Chapter 33

BLUNDERS AT THE BIBLE BAPTIST CHURCH

ONE SUNDAY, we had an unbelievable guest. I've always heard the saying, "Blind as a bat," but don't remember ever seeing one until that Sunday morning. It flew back and forth across the room and one of our men, Retus Humble, grabbed a broom hoping to swat it out the door. After several minutes, he won the battle of pest control!

In the same building, we bought a new, forced-air furnace and didn't have money for duct work. Instead, we just set it up on the concrete floor and hooked it up. When we got to church, we turned on the thermostat and, a few minutes later, it would start and blow warm air throughout the building. One cold Sunday morning, we arrived at church and turned it on and started our song service. In the middle of one of the hymns, we heard a loud bumping noise and wondered what in the world could be going wrong. Out of the furnace ran a scared, furless cat! It had just had the most thrilling ride of its life. Evidently, he had crawled up in the squirrel cage fan that was in the heater and fallen asleep. When the blower came on, he had a rude awakening!

Another Sunday morning, we all met together singing and, all at once, the church door came open, and what we thought was a machine gun began firing. Everyone went to the floor under the pews. When the noise subsided, we were surprised to see a teenager, who had been sitting at the back of the church when the door opened, Danny Gross, standing alive and well! We soon discovered a string of firecracker debris left behind by an unknown person. Danny sure kept calm in the line of fire! All is well that ends well.

Chapter 34

BRO. BILL LOVES HIS CARS

Therefore if any man be in Christ, he is a new creature:
Old things are passed away; behold, all things are become new.

(2 CORINTHIANS 5:17)

M Y VERY FIRST CAR, a 1946 Plymouth, was given to me by my father right before Norma and I were married in 1955. Two years later, while working at Eureka Motor Company, we purchased a 1952 Dodge. We were so poor that when the brakes would go out on one wheel, I would use a hammer and smash the brake line to that wheel, and then we would only have brakes on three wheels. When the same thing happened on another wheel, I got out the hammer and then had brakes on two wheels. When the master-cylinder started leaking in the summertime and I couldn't afford brake fluid, I used water instead and it worked! I must admit I was a poor preacher. Thank the Lord for our overworked guardian angels!

Soon after I accepted the pastorate of the Prescott Baptist Church, I went to work for the Kipper Chevrolet-Oldsmobile dealer in Pleasanton, Kansas, eight miles from Prescott. Jim Kipper was the owner and he sold me a beautiful, one-owner 1955 Oldsmobile at a good price. It was so nice, like a new car. I drove it for three years, until we moved to Dodge City, Kansas.

†

While pastoring the church in Dodge City, I had the best job I had ever had outside of the ministry. Gerald Bailes owned the Dodge City Salvage Yard, and we developed a wonderful lifelong relationship. Mr. Bailes always treated me like a son, and he became one of my dearest friends. From then on, I never lacked a car to drive! I would see a totaled car brought in by a wrecker and I would fall in love with it. My boss would sell it to me for just what it cost him. I'd rent a small garage and start working on my new project late at night.

Often, I would think it was ten o'clock at night, and it would end up being two o'clock in the morning. Time would fly and I was having fun! Thank the Lord for a long-suffering wife taking care of our six little children and never complained about me being gone so much. I was able to buy plenty of parts from the wrecking yard and Mr. Bailes would sell them to me at cost. Then the exciting day would come and I would pay a body shop to paint my new car. This process continued from one car to the next. For the next six years, while I worked for Mr. Bailes, most of the cars I rebuilt were nice, late-model, low-mileage cars. When Billy, my son, became a teenager, it was my joy to help him rebuild cars—among them a Dukes of Hazard Dodge and a Camaro!

Now the day came when the church grew large enough to give me a full-time salary, but I shall never forget those wrecked, twisted cars that I saw transformed. When they came in, they seemed without hope, and after lots of work they looked brand new. It reminds me of lives that I've seen Jesus transform. What joy was brought to our family when we were able to drive one of those new vehicles.

†

In 1949, my mom and dad were finally able to buy a nice vehicle: A 1946 Model T Ford. My parents lovingly let me drive it five miles into Fredonia to try to get a date for a school function. The speedometer cable was broken and I was driving too fast. I lost control. I rolled the car end over end and it landed on its top. I crawled out the window and Bud Clary, our neighbor, came out of his house to see what happened. I asked him to get his tractor and roll the car back over and I would get it home. He said, "I won't touch the car util I talk to your dad!"

The last person I wanted to face was my father! I had received many spankings in my life and I knew that this was one I sure deserved. Bud drove me to our house in his pickup and we told my father that I had ruined his new car—his pride and joy! How would he respond?

He asked me how I was feeling. He was only thinking of me and if I was hurt. I was fine except I had some sand and broken glass in my hair. And then I heard the sweetest words my father could have ever spoken: "Son, don't worry about the fool car, we can replace it, but we can't replace you!" How sweet to be forgiven!

He insisted that I drive the farm pickup the very next day. I can see the Lord's hand in the whole thing, because even though the girl I was going to ask out was a sweet, Christian girl, the Lord had a better choice waiting for me!

†

In 1981, one of the greatest surprises of my life was on a Sunday morning after church. Bro. Richard Buchanan said, "Bro. Bill, we want you and Norma to come out in front of the church." We went out, and there sat a beautiful, brand-new Ford Fairmont! They said, "This is yours." I don't know how they raised that much money for such a beautiful car. I am now eighty-five years old, and it's the only brand-new car I have ever owned!

Psalms 37:25 says, "I have been young, and now am old; yet have I not seen the righteous forsaken, nor his seed begging bread." God has been so good to me!

Dodge City – TV Altar, 1963

Dodge City Congregation, 1969

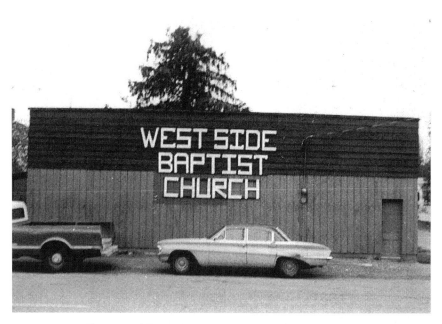

First Building, Westside Baptist Church, 1969

Bloom Youth Camp, 1970

Bro. Bill Wambsganss Family, 1970

Moving Westside Baptist Building, 1971

Dodge City – TV Altar, 1971

Preaching from the Rooftop, 1972

Old-fashioned Sunday, 1973

Phillip, Leon, Becky, Stephen, and Andrew Wambsganss, 1976

Bro. Leslie Baker, Missionary to Haiti, 1976

1980s

Chapter 35

ISAAC KOPPEL'S GIFT

*So built we the wall; and all the wall was joined together
unto the half thereof; for the people had a mind to work.*

(NEHEMIAH 4:6)

WHILE MY DAD WAS PASTORING at the Westside Baptist Church in Bremerton, Washington, the building that had been given to the church by the funeral home was great for Sunday school, but the church was growing and needed an auditorium. The Lord provided an unexpected gift through an unexpected person.

Now, my father had a gift of seeing each individual as a soul in need of a Savior! Their financial status or their mental capabilities made no difference to him. One day as he was knocking on doors, he came to a humble, little house and met a cordial man with special needs and his kind mother. The man's name was Isaac Koppel.

Because of Isaac's disability, he was able to get a job at the Navy shipyard under the special needs program. It was difficult to communicate with him, but he was able to push a broom at the Naval shipyard. When dad offered to pick them up and bring them to church, they consented and became regular attenders.

After a couple of years, his mother went to a rest home and, after a while, Isaac had to retire due to health reasons. My dad would faithfully pick up Isaac and bring him to church services until he was no longer able to attend. Every week, my dad would go by the house to check on Isaac.

One day when my dad went by to visit, he knocked on the door and there was no answer. They got permission for the police to break into the house from Isaac's nephew, who was a doctor in Seattle. They found that Isaac had passed away about three days before.

Through the years, Isaac had regularly invested most of his earnings in CD's in the bank. So, when his family went through his belongings, they found a will that said, "When I'm gone, if my mother is still alive, I want her taken care of. After that, I want everything that's left to go to Westside Baptist Church." Isaac's mother lived about two more years. After his final expenses were paid, and the very small house was sold, there was approximately $70,000 that was left to Westside Baptist Church.

The church was so thankful to the Lord for this unexpected gift. My dad used that large gift to start a building campaign to build a new auditorium. The church began with $1000. Different members of the church would promise to take a specific month to give over and above their regular tithes and offerings. Through that time of sacrifice, they raised $70,000 and then borrowed another $70,000 from the bank.

The whole church congregation was so inspired by the challenge of the much needed new church building that the men of the church did the construction, working long hours every day and into the night. The ladies would bring food and take care of the church visitations so that the men could focus on the building. When the new building was completed, there was certainly much rejoicing for Westside Baptist as well!

Once again, our great God used the inspiration of an unlikely man to do what seemed impossible to man. Because of his physical limitations, Bro. Isaac Koppel could not teach a Sunday school class, or preach a sermon, or even sing in the choir, but he did what he could, and dozens of others followed his example and greatly sacrificed.

Because of their labor of love, in the years that have followed, scores of people have trusted Christ and many are already in heaven. Still today, souls are being saved and lives transformed because of their faithful service.

What a thrill and demonstration of God's grace that my father was able to see the project completed. He was able to celebrate the dedication of the building and preach in it for several months before God seemed to say, "You've finished the course. Well done my good and faithful servant."

Chapter 36

DAD'S HOMEGOING

And as it is appointed unto man once to die,
but after this the judgment.

(HEBREWS 9:27)

But none of these things move me, neither count I my life
dear unto myself, so that I might finish my course with joy,
and the ministry, which I have received of the
Lord Jesus, to testify the Gospel of the grace of God.

(ACTS 20:24)

MY FATHER NEVER SANG IN PUBLIC, but when I was young, I could hear him on the farm as he worked the horses in the field, half a mile away. I'm sure this song was his theme and testimony:

> *This world is not my home I'm just a passing through.*
> *My treasures are laid up somewhere beyond the blue.*
> *The angels beckon' me from heaven's open door*
> *and I can't feel at home in this world anymore*

My dad knew he was getting older. He was in his late 60s and had regular doctor's visits. One day, he talked to me about his death and I said, "Dad, don't talk like that." He replied, "I know my station in life and God told us to count our days." He knew that life was uncertain and that death was sure.

It was Friday, July 9, after picking beans in his garden, that my father went home to heaven. The day before, he had preached and recorded the first sermon on his new radio program that was to play that Sunday morning: *Prepare to Meet Thy God.* It was the last sermon he would ever preach. In the sermon, he said, "My wife and I travel often, but before going we always plan and prepare for our trip." What a God-given title . . . what good advice for all of us to heed!

When I heard the news, I was at a local paint store buying paint for our Bloom, Kansas youth camp when the manager of the store said, "Bro. Bill, you're wanted on the store telephone." (Most people knew me in Dodge City as Bro. Bill and many watched *TV Altar.*) My wife, Norma, was on the other end of the phone. She told me that my father had just had a massive heart attack and had gone to be with the Lord.

My next stop was our local credit union, where I borrowed $1,000. Then, I called my brother, Leon, in Texas. We made flight arrangements to meet in Denver and fly together from there to the Seattle airport to be with our mother. Evelyn and Paul came as soon as they could.

Without a doubt, the greatest day of my father's life was when he was born again at twenty-four years of age. His life was never the same again. His greatest joy in life was sharing with others about that wonderful day. For the Christian, death is not the end, but the best is yet to come! The best gift you can leave for your grieving family is the promise of a great family reunion in heaven for those who are prepared, because we have all sinned and need a Savior.

What a day July 9 must have been for dad! Like when Stephen died, I imagine that Jesus was standing there welcoming him home. What a day that will be when we join him with the Heavenly Father in heaven forever. Dad certainly fought a good fight, finished the course, and kept the faith.

What a challenge for us to be sure that we are prepared to meet our Lord and our loved ones in heaven, being sure that Jesus is our Savior! *What a day that will be!* It may be sooner than you think! Are you sure you're ready? Romans 10:13 says, "For whosoever shall call upon the name of the Lord shall be saved."

Many funerals are sad, but because of his testimony, my dad's was a joyous time. For we know "to be absent from the body is to be present with the Lord." We are so thankful that he didn't have to suffer, and we were so honored for the hundreds who came and showed their love and respect for him at the Bremerton, Washington service. A second service was also held at our home church at Bible Baptist Church in Fredonia, Kansas. He was buried in our family plot in Toronto, Kansas next to my brother, Donnie. A few years later, my mother joined dad in heaven and is also buried there now.

My dad left us a good spiritual inheritance and so many wonderful memories. Oh, that the same could be said of us. Success in life cannot be measured in dollars, or fame, or fortune, but to live as the apostle Paul lived. Philippians 1:21 says, "For me to live is Christ, and to die is gain."

Acts 4:12 reads, "Neither is there salvation in any other: for there is none other name under heaven given among men, whereby we must be saved." What a thrill it is to see the many lives that were touched and changed through his ministry. Even after my father's death, the radio ministry continued on at Westside Baptist Church. He and Bro. Kearns set a great foundation. Forty-three years of faithful service to the Lord! It continues to this very day in the lives of fellow saints and family members. And it will continue until Jesus comes back again.

I remember standing with my father at my grandfather's grave when he said, "I am next." Now I am echoing those words. I'm next in line, unless Jesus comes first. I thank the Lord for a godly dad. I look forward to that great family reunion in heaven. I hope there won't be any empty chairs around the table. Now is the time to make your reservation sure. There's still room! As Ira Stanphill wrote in his great song,

> *There's room at the cross for you. There's room at the cross for you.*
> *Though millions have come, there's still room for one.*
> *Yes, there's room at the cross for you!*

Chapter 37

FOLLOWING IN DAD'S FOOTSTEPS TO BREMERTON, WASHINGTON

WHILE I WAS IN BREMERTON for my father's funeral, the men of the church approached me and asked me if I wanted to candidate for the church. I told them it would be alright, but I wouldn't come to try out. With my dad pastoring there for more than twelve years, I had preached there many times, and I felt like they knew me inside and out.

After the funeral, I went home to Dodge City, Kansas and, within a couple of weeks, they called me and said the church had voted for me to be their pastor. My heart was filled with mixed emotions. For over twenty-two years, we had served in Dodge City. We were content there and the Lord had richly blessed. We lived in a large, beautiful parsonage, and all of our six children and grandchildren were in Dodge City.

The parsonage in Bremerton was an old, four-room house that my dad had bought for $1.00 at an auction. We had a nice building in Dodge City, and Bremerton had just completed their brand-new building, with the help of Isaac Koppel.

I can't imagine the feelings that were going through Norma's heart. Moving so far away from our children, grandchildren, and our comfortable house had to have been so difficult. I now know how my parents must have felt when they moved so far away.

Kissing, hugging, and waving goodbye to our children and grandkids was not easy. The day came when two men from the Bremerton church came to help us drive the U-Haul, with all of our belongings, to Washington. We drove for three long days, trying to figure out where we would put all of our stuff inside that tiny, four-room house. The church had an enclosed bus barn, so when we arrived, we were able to store some of our excess belongings there.

Our youngest daughter, Betty Jo, was the only one who moved with us. What a trooper Betty was. She never complained about leaving the only city and schools she had ever known. She still had two years left in high school, but she settled right in! We enrolled her in Bremerton Christian School, and what a blessing it was to see her flourish as she easily made new friends.

In order to make room for us, my brother, Leon, had flown up from Texas and bought a small mobile home for my mother. He moved it in on the backside of the church property, behind the small parsonage. My mother missed my father so much that we counted more than thirty pictures of him throughout her mobile home. He was her one-and-only, the love of her life.

Even though she dearly missed him, she felt his ministry must go on. She dearly loved the people and they loved her! Early every morning, she would go down the hill to her church office in the new building and brew a fresh pot of coffee, read her Bible, and eat a piece or two of candy from her stash. Men of the church would drop by just to say "hi" and have a fresh cup of coffee. I think the church ran on coffee!

My mother felt needed and, every Saturday, would prepare a delicious breakfast for the Sunday school bus workers before they went out to visit the children on their bus routes. She was always available during the day to give advice and old-fashioned home remedies to the young mothers of the church. She also answered the church phone.

During my father's ministry, he hand wrote every sermon he preached from his private study: a small camping trailer parked in a quiet place at the back of the church property. It was an ideal place for him to study and pray. When his sermon was ready, my mother would type it up for him. Often, my father would attend pastors' meetings and my mother would always write down the sermon outlines so that my dad could go home and add them to the 30+ years of outlines he already had. After dad's death, she used every spare moment going through them and compiling the ones she thought would especially remind us of him. She made copies and bought three-ring notebooks, giving them to family, pastors, and friends.

Norma was also immensely used by the Lord there with her musical abilities. In addition to many ladies' activities, she started a lady's ensemble and worked with groups for special music. She also had a monthly ladies' meeting, as well as a yearly ladies' retreat at a resort on the coast.

My mother and my wife were best friends and pastors' wives. Even though they deeply loved each other, I'm sure at first the adjustment was hard on Norma: one church with two pastors' wives. But they were both so loving and gracious! The church was blessed to have both of their gifts and ministries.

Chapter 38

EVELYN'S LOSS: TONY AND TIMMY MUSGROVE

Many things about tomorrow I don't seem to understand,
but I know who holds tomorrow and I know who holds my
hand. The God of the mountain is still God in the valley.
Casting all your care upon him; for he careth for you.

(1 PETER 5:7)

EVEN JESUS WEPT AT LAZARUS'S GRAVE; He fills our life with joys and tears. I'm so thankful He's always there, especially in times of need!

When my father was pastoring The Bible Baptist Church in Independence, Kansas, my sweet sister, Evelyn, married Carl Musgrove. When Carl and Evelyn were first married, Carl joined the military and was stationed down south. Evelyn came to live with Norma and me in Eureka, Kansas. She attended high school while she was with us, finishing her courses and getting her GED. When Carl got out of the military, they moved to Independence, Kansas. Evelyn continued her education at Kansas State Teacher's College in Pittsburg, Kansas and went on to receive a master's degree. She was hired at the Independence Junior College to teach psychology.

God blessed Carl and Evelyn with four great sons: Timmy, Terry, Tony, and Todd. Their oldest son, Timmy, came to our youth camp at Bloom, Kansas with his friend, Danny Bentz, who became part of their family and still is today. Both surrendered to preach while at the camp.

Timmy married Rosie Bayes on August 21, 1977, and, soon after, enrolled at Southwest Baptist University in Boliver, Missouri. After completing his Biblical studies, he accepted the call to pastor the Baptist church in Sedan, Kansas.

On the Friday night of November 4, 1983, one of Evelyn's other sons, Tony, was in a hurry to pick up his fiancé for a ballgame. On the way, Tony met a school bus at a sharp corner in the road. Swerving to miss it, he lost control of the car and was killed. What a heartbreaking tragedy! Everyone loved Tony. Carl and Evelyn's hearts were broken. I flew back from Washington state for his funeral to grieve with the family. But we don't grieve as others that have no hope! Tony knew the Lord and we knew there would be a reunion day with him. What a hard valley that was for my sister and her family.

After the funeral, his big brother, Timmy, asked me to come out to his car and to listen to a sermon on cassette tape. The title was "The Cry of the Unborn," a message about abortion. I had no idea that this would be the last interaction I would ever have with Timmy.

On December 20, 1983, just six weeks after his brother Tony's death, Timmy was returning home from Independence Junior College where he was working part-time as he pastored. There was a bad snow storm and he needed to get home to his wife, Rosie, and his two little boys, Nathan and Jeremy, who were in Sedan, Kansas, just thirty-six miles away. It was five days before Christmas. Evelyn had just told her son goodbye and to be careful. He had a lot to do because this Christmas was going to be very different: his little brother, Tony, would be missing from their family gathering.

From what we know, it seems like a vehicle came out of nowhere as Timmy was trying to pass a car ahead of him. His wife, mother, and family were not prepared for the news: Rosie, Nathan, and Jeremy lost their husband and daddy—right before Christmas. In only six weeks, my sister, Evelyn, lost two of her four sons. They must have wondered if the sun would ever shine again? But God is faithful: *I will never leave thee or forsake thee.* (Hebrews 13:5)

I cannot even imagine what it would be like to lose a child, let alone two children in a month's time. Evelyn and Carl were so strong throughout this awful, shocking, and painful event. But I know from speaking with both of them, what got them through it was trusting in the Lord and clinging to him. God provided such great encouragement as family and friends prayed for strength.

Life does continue and God still had great plans ahead for my sister's family. Evelyn and Carl's two remaining sons faithfully serve the Lord: Terry, in Ponca City, Oklahoma, and Todd and his son, Josh, in Dixon, Illinois. Danny Bentz, Timmy's friend from camp, and his wife, Bert, are in Dixon, Illinois where Danny has pastored the Northside Baptist Church for over thirty-six years. What an encouragement to see his faithfulness in ministry these many years.

Timmy's widow, Rosie, re-married Dale Sweaney on March 29, 1986. They have a son, Phillip, born January 31, 1988. Dale and Rosie have faithfully served in the Baptist Church in Sedan, Kansas where once Timmy pastored. Rosie retired from teaching music in public schools and is still a great pianist.

My sister's tragedy, her love of the Lord, and her education made a perfect mix for God to use her to help hurting people! What thrilling memories we have of such a strong lady. Evelyn and Carl couldn't have made it without the Lord.

Chapter 39

BACK TO HAITI

THE TRIP WITH MY SON BILLY wasn't the end of my trips to Haiti, it was just the beginning! Soon after I moved to Bremerton, two of the men in the church, Chuck Morris and Terry Prost, accompanied me to visit Bro. Baker and take several bicycles for his fellow pastors there. Our purpose for being at the mission station was to help them build a new church building.

Bro. Baker's personal living conditions were so primitive. The paths that he had to drive his jeep on were scary, to say the least! He loaded us up in his jeep for a trip north to one of his remote mission stations, and we had to stop at a military check station to get permission to pass on. When we finally arrived, we were given a little shack about twelve square feet with a dirt floor and walls made out of sticks and dried mud. Up the wall ran a chameleon adapting its color to its background. Bro. Chuck Morris, the treasurer of our church and a man of few words said to me, "Pastor, I wasn't expecting much, but this is ridiculous!"

There was no lumber available, so they cut down trees and used their machetes to shave off the round part of the log. They would stand the logs up and bury them in a hole they had dug. Fastening the log crossways, they built something similar to a pole barn in the U.S. It was so amazing to see what they could do with so little resources! About the only thing that would have to be brought in from civilization was the corrugated metal sheets for the roof. Indeed, the building was crude, but it provided shelter from the rain. Because of the tropical climate, heating and air-conditioning were not needed. The building was well on its way to being completed when we left, and people walked twenty miles to spend all day at church.

It was a trip to be remembered! Seeing how our missionaries lived in Haiti sure helped us know how to pray for them. The people there are so poor, but you'll not find a happier group! Their love for the Lord has carried them through hurricanes and earthquakes.

And even though it was colder back in Washington, it was great to be home in the United States of America!

Chapter 40

FUNNY BAPTISM STORIES

GETTING BAPTIZED IS always an exciting time in people's lives! Early in my ministry, our church didn't have a baptistery, so we would go out to the river to baptize. After the people were baptized they would hold up blankets to shield themselves from view while they changed into dry clothes. We would sing *Shall We Gather at the River* and people would shout out, "Praise the Lord!"

At a city-wide meeting we had in Junction City, Kansas with Bro. Art Wilson, many people were saved. Bro. Art contacted the pastor of an African American congregation and got permission to baptize the new converts in their church building. I was the song leader, and *my* ... how the congregation could sing! They got me excited, and I was walking all over the platform—the back side of that platform was level with the baptismal tank. As I backed up, I almost got baptized too!

Years later, on a trip to Haiti with Bro. Baker, I had the privilege of going to a river baptism for many Haitians that had been saved. They had a custom that was unusual, and I thought it was neat. All that came to be baptized were dressed in white. I don't remember them changing out of their wet clothes because Haiti is so tropical. There was much rejoicing and everyone was so joyful!

For my first nine years of being a pastor in Dodge City, Kansas, we didn't have a baptistery. I remember one of the times we went to a lake that was north of town. By the time we arrived at the lake, our people were weary and the cars were covered with dust from the dirt road. And then the worst came: When we walked out into the lake we were half-way up to our knees in mud, but thank the Lord, we made it! It is indelibly written on that page of our memory.

I remember another incident when one of our bus children was saved and, with permission from his parents, was going to be baptized. He came into the baptistery and before I knew it, he was swimming across! It took me by surprise. You never knew what to expect, but we did get him baptized.

In Bremerton, Washington we had a thriving deaf department in the church. There was a most eccentric man in his thirties, Robert Roach, who trusted Jesus as his Savior, despite having mental disabilities. When I looked up and saw him walking down the steps into the baptistery, there he was— with swimming goggles and a snorkel! We managed to get him baptized without the extra gear.

One of the Navy men in our church, Steve Kirkham, invited his officer, Glen Stegel, to church. Glenn accepted the Lord as his Savior and requested to be baptized out in open water like Jesus had been. We took him outside of town, and he was baptized in the bay. He became a godly testimony.

Chapter 41

LEE EVERETT

NOT EVERYONE THAT RODE the Sunday school buses were children . . . some were adults. Among them was a single man about forty years old named Lee Everett. Lee was always happy and very proud of his Native American heritage as part of the Blackfoot tribe. Everybody loved him and Bro. Corey Higdon, his bus captain, nicknamed him Bro. Ever-ready because when the bus would arrive at his house, he was always ready!

After church services one Sunday evening we all ate watermelon in the church yard. We looked over and Lee was slumped in his chair. Someone quickly called 911 and when the ambulance arrived, they said he was gone. What better place to go to heaven than from the house of God? Lee rode the bus to church and the angels carried him home to heaven.

George Wambsganss giving office furniture to Bro. Bill

Dr. and Mrs. George Wambsganss, 1982

1990s

Chapter 42

NORMA'S ILLNESS

Her children rise up and call her blessed.

(PROVERBS 31:28)

IT WAS A SAD DAY DURING the Spring of 1992 when we found out that the love of my life, my beloved wife and partner, Norma Luella Smith Wambsganss had breast cancer. Norma had gone for her yearly doctor's appointment, and a mammogram determined that she had a small lump. The doctor wanted to watch it and have it checked again. In six months, the lump had really grown, and we had to make the decision whether Norma would have a lumpectomy or a mastectomy. After talking with the doctor, our kids, and much prayer, we decided on a lumpectomy.

At that time, our great kids decided that their mother needed help. All of our girls lived in Dallas, Texas and had good careers with the YMCA. Beth was an essential staff at the YMCA, but decided it was more important to move to Washington to help care for her mother. The other five children band together and committed to financially support Beth so she could still take care of her bills while caring for Norma. That was such a blessing.

After the lumpectomy in the Fall of 1992, Norma started chemotherapy and radiation. It took a lot out of her, but even while hosting missionaries, visitations, and special music at the church, she never complained once and continued to be the best mom and pastor's wife you could imagine.

Even so, in the Spring of 1993, Norma started feeling worse. We found out the cancer had come back with a vengeance, so immediately a mastectomy was performed. It was determined that Beth needed help, so Betty Jo left her job to move to Washington and be with her mom as well.

119

Norma was an amazing helpmate. She was always thinking of others instead of herself. I remember that, right after the mastectomy, I was the main speaker for a youth camp in Colorado. Norma was still feeling poorly, but she insisted on accompanying me to the youth camp. It was a very hard trip for her. She still had a drain tube in her side and was in a lot of pain. Later, she told me that she would not have changed a thing. Her priority was the ministry and that souls would be saved in the youth camp. She didn't want to miss out on being part of that.

Although Beth and Betty took such good care of her—dressing her up on Sundays, putting her in the wheelchair, taking her to church—she never fully recovered after the mastectomy. Even when Norma was feeling her worst, she was concerned about things like towels at the church for baptism, and that there were meals prepared for myself, guest pastors, and missionaries. Through it all, she was just the best pastor's wife you could imagine.

In February of 1994, the doctor told us that nothing else could be done to save her life. What a sad day. We called and told all the kids. Our son, Bill, who was also living in Washington, was such a help during this difficult time. Becky, Bonnie, and Brenda were all in Dallas, but came to visit their mother one last time. They all said how difficult it was to leave their mother knowing they would never see her again on earth.

On April 15, 1994, at the age of 63, Norma went to heaven to meet her Lord. We know her mother, Sylvia Smith, was waiting at heaven's gate to welcome her sweet daughter. All of the kids from Dallas jumped in their cars and headed to Bremerton, Washington for the funeral where hundreds of family and friends gathered to remember my godly wife, Norma Wambsganss. I was so blessed to have her by my side for thirty-nine years. The Lord is good!

Chapter 43

SHARON BATES

The Lord knows the way through the wilderness,
all I have to do is follow.

AT ONE OF OUR WASHINGTON STATE pastors' fellowship meetings, I was visiting with Pastor Ralph Bates from the Goldendale Baptist Church. He told me that a week earlier he had been changing oil in his car and, out of nowhere, had severe pain. The next day, he went to the doctor and the diagnosis was that he had cancer with only three months to three years to live. He looked like the picture of health, but from that time on he went downhill. A few months later, he went home to be with the Lord. Many pastor friends attended his funeral in Spokane, Washington. He was buried in a family plot in the bay area of California that overlooks the Golden Gate Bridge.

When Ralph died, my wife Norma had been battling breast cancer for two years but would only live another five months. After some time, several pastors suggested that I should meet Sharon Bates, Ralph's widow. Several months later, I called and asked Sharon if she would like to go to dinner with me. I drove across the state to Spokane, and we went out to the Olive Garden. We enjoyed each other's friendship and shared how we were dealing with the death of our spouses. After that, we tried to see each other every month at the pastors' fellowship meetings. When I finally popped the question, she asked, "Are you certain that it is the Lord's will?" I said yes and she said yes!

Sharon had two grown children, Brian and Sheree. Sharon talked to them and got their blessing, and I did the same with my six children. The wedding day was set, although when I suggested April 1, she declined.

We were married on April 7, 1995, in the church building in Bremerton, Washington. Sharon's pastor from Spokane and her brother, Roger Frye, officiated the ceremony. Many family members from both sides attended and were involved, as well as a host of friends. My two youngest daughters, Beth and Betty Jo, paid for our honeymoon to the Bahamas—and what a trip it was!

Upon our return, Sharon settled in as the pastor's wife of the Westside Baptist Church. For the next seven years, she hosted ladies' fellowships and retreats, as well as singing specials. During those years we traveled to youth camps in Colorado, Texas, British Columbia, and Canada. We also took missionary trips to England, Romania, and a very special trip to the Holy Land.

One of our most exciting trips was going to England and visit Dr. Stephen Wray, a University Professor in Victoria, British Columbia, who had accepted the Lord and surrendered to go back to his home country of England to be a missionary. Our church had agreed to be his sending church when he and his family traveled through the U.S. on deputation. After being there a couple of years, our church voted to send me and Sharon to Leeds in order to visit them. My brother, Leon, who had had spent a lot of time in England with his Accent International Radio Spanish ministry, volunteered to meet us and drive us around. He was a master at driving on the wrong side of the street! I would have had a wreck my first time around the block. But Leon drove us from London to Leeds.

We attended church on a Sunday and enjoyed Bro. Wray, as he was a good saxophone player, and his wife was an accomplished violin and piano player. During our week, we stayed in a nice bed and breakfast with all kinds of exotic foods, even blood pudding.

During the day, we would go to downtown Leeds. It was a large town, and most of the streets were narrow and made for walking. Bro. Wray, his oldest son, a preacher friend of his, and I would take turns preaching on these streets, while the rest of us passed out tracts. One of our group would wear a sandwich board that had scripture verses printed on the back. Speaking on the streets was a common thing for cults, political people, etc., and the streets were loaded with people.

Side trips with the Wrays included a magnificent cathedral and a very large outdoor zoo. At the end of our visit with the Wrays, Leon picked us up in the rental car and took us several miles away to a World War II headquarters building where he rented a place to store his radio recording equipment. There were many memorials of World War II all over England.

Sharon and I sure enjoyed our trip to England and the Wray family's hospitality!

I pastored Westside Baptist Church in Bremerton, Washington a total of twenty years—what a blessing it was! Bremerton has a Navy base and so, it was my privilege to pastor a lot of Navy families. What a joy! The Navy guys had so much energy and were so willing to work and help grow the church. Our members were more than willing to work hard and get done anything that I needed help with. I made many life-long friends there and it was very hard for me to leave them. What an honor to pastor the church my dad had pastored before me! I had invited a young evangelist, Craig Houston, to come hold a revival for our church in 2002. When I resigned at the age of sixty-seven, Bro. Craig was called as the new pastor. Although it was hard to leave, I knew the Lord had other things in store for us. We were off to the next stage of life . . .

Sharon and I had recently purchased a nice, used motor home. Although we weren't homeless, it was certainly not easy to leave the people we loved and the beautiful parsonage. We really believed it was God's will and that's what mattered. The Lord knew the thrills that were ahead that we could not yet see. We were as free as birds to do revivals, youth camps, and filling pulpits when pastors were out of town.

On December 11, 2016, Sharon was reunited with her first love, Ralph, in heaven. Sharon's two sweet children were by her side when she went to be with the Lord. She was buried next to Ralph in El Cerate, California. My son, Bill, and daughters, Becky and Beth, drove to California to be with me for the burial. Bonnie, Brenda, and Betty Jo had flown to Spokane for the funeral there.

The Lord gave Sharon and me twenty-one years of wonderful memories and precious promises. Sharon was a wonderful helpmate. I'm so thankful

123

the Lord had a plan for us to meet and that we were able to share those years together! Thank God for his plans, his presence, and his provisions. *Great is thy faithfulness!* And the best is yet to come!

After the burial in California, I was willingly kidnapped to Texas to start the next chapter of my life.

Chapter 44

TO HAITI AGAIN WITH KEITH BATES

BLENDED FAMILIES CAN present challenges, but in my experience, it was a great blessing! When Sharon and I got married, I inherited six wonderful step-grandchildren: Melody, Karrisa, Koreen, Greg, Jordan, and Keith.

So, when Bro. Baker invited me to come to Haiti again to hold a youth camp for him, I asked Keith to come with me. He already had a deep interest in serving the Lord and had helped me at a youth camp in Colorado.

Keith has a very light complexion and red hair, while most Haitians are from African descent. He definitely stood out, but he was a teenager that loved the Lord! And Keith had no problem eating anything they offered him!

When we arrived in Port-au-Prince, we visited several of Bro. Baker's missions, pastor friends, and also his Bible college for training national workers. Rules for driving a car there seemed to be much different than in the U.S. For example, the first one to an intersection has the right-of-way, unless the car coming from the other way has the loudest horn. So what did Bro. Baker do? He got his little jeep a loud air horn like the big trucks use! Most of the time, he got the right-of-way.

After days of ministry and fellowship in the big city, Bro. Baker took Keith and I back to the airport where he had rented a missionary aircraft plane and a pilot to fly us deep into the interior to the campsite. The pilot, along with the three of us, filled the plane, and Keith filmed the whole trip with a camcorder. When we arrived at our destination, the little village didn't have an airport so we landed in a pasture. But there was a problem . . . there were cattle and horses where we needed to land. In order for us to land, the pilot had to buzz down close so that he could chase the animals away.

It so happened that our trip was during the Haitian Mardi Gras. It was weird to hear the voodoo drums echoing in the distance at night, but Bro. Baker had several voodoo witch doctors accept Christ under his ministry. In the village, they had a large tent-like meeting place set up. Many of the non-Christian Haitians gathered together, dressed in all kinds of wild costumes, and marched up to where we were having services, chanting as they went. They probably wanted to disturb us, but bold Bro. Baker was not shaken, and we continued with our worship of the Lord!

How exciting it was to hear those Haitians sing! You can really tell that they love the Lord. I watched one of Keith's videos of the Haitians asking Bro. Baker to sing a special. You could tell it was from his heart! My how he loved the Lord and those Haitian people. Keith also got to sing and, even at his young age, he was already a great singer. I got to do what I love best and tell Bible stories to young people. Back in Port-au-Prince, Keith met a young man that had volunteered to help another missionary there in Haiti, and they became best friends.

After returning home, Keith graduated from Heartland Bible Baptist College in Oklahoma City where he met and married my grand-niece, Julie Smith, Leo Smith's grand-daughter. After those boys were both married, and Keith had become a pastor in Colorado, Keith's church supported his friend as a missionary to Haiti.

Keith and Julie have eight children now, and he has pastored in Penrose, Colorado for years—and you should hear his children sing! They call themselves the B Sisters: Next Generation. I love that!

What a blessing to see the family heritage continue!

Chapter 45

THE BATES FAMILY

I'm so glad I'm a part of the family of God.

S HARON'S MOTHER AND FATHER, Mom and Dad Lawson, were
dedicated Christians. Sharon's children, Brian and Sheree', were
always wonderful to me and, most of all, they loved the Lord. Brian's wife,
Leslie, was also such a blessing, as well as all of my "new" grandchildren.
Sharon's mom, Mom Lawson, taught Sunday school and read her Bible
through each year for over fifty years.

Sharon's family, like my own, is very musical and grew up singing
together in church. It was a great part of their lives. I remember we took
a trip with Mom Lawson to the ocean and on the way home, we sang one
hymn after another for over 100 miles. We would meet at Mom Lawson's
house one night a week to play UNO. Mom Lawson usually won!

During our motorhome days, we would have extended stays at Mom
Lawson's home, Brian and Leslie's home, and Sharee's home. We were
always made to feel so loved and accepted.

It was a sad day when Dad Lawson passed away. A few years later,
Mom Lawson also went home to be with the Lord. It was a thrill at each
of their services to hear how God had blessed others through their lives.

Sharon's daughter, Sheree', lived about three miles away from us and
was a tremendous help to us as Sharon's health began to decline. We were
so blessed that Brian, Sharon's son now living in Colorado, was able to
return and be by Sharon's side in the hospital the night she went to heaven.

I feel the Lord's been so good to me, and the Bates family has been
such a blessing from God. I hope and pray that we'll all be together in
heaven.

Chapter 46

HONORARY DOCTORATES

SOON AFTER NORMA PASSED AWAY, pastor friends and college admin-
istrators honored me with a Doctor of Divinity degree from Pacific
Coast Baptist Bible College at San Dimas, California. My two youngest
daughters, Beth and Betty Jo, had graduated from there several years
before. Sharon, my mother, and Steve Kirkham, the assistant pastor with
me at Westside Baptist, flew to California for the presentation.

My brother, Leon, flew from Texas to California and, without me
knowing, rented a Cadillac to chauffeur us in style to and from the presentation. It was very kind of the college to honor me with the degree. I've
never used the title Doctor . . . because no one likes Doctor Bills!

Earlier, Leon had given me and my father Doctor of Divinity degrees
from the Bible Baptist Seminary of Madrid, Spain.

I returned to Bremerton feeling very loved and appreciated. It was a
very kind gesture.

Chapter 47

BIBLE SCHOOLS AND YOUTH CAMPS

And Jesus called a little child unto him, and set him in the midst of them, And said, Verily I say unto you, Except ye be converted and become as little children, ye shall not enter into the kingdom of heaven.

(MATTHEW 18:2-3)

JESUS ALWAYS HAD A TENDER spot for children! During the summers, I would often be asked to speak at youth camps and vacation bible schools. I loved children and worked to make bible characters and stories come to life for them. Norma had a love for camps too, and would almost always accompany me on those trips. We would occasionally take Jeremy Rabe, our oldest grandchild, with us. During our time in Dodge City, when we had the Bloom youth camps, Norma was the chief cook and would prepare three meals a day for the pastors and the kids who attended, as well as be in charge of clean-up. She always had a great team to help her!

After moving to Washington, two of my great friends from Kansas had camp ministries. Bro. Lloyd Gross had Silver State Youth Camp, a camp that Bro. Harvey Springer started in Colorado. Greg Waggoner hosted a camp called Hidden Valley Camp in the Amarillo, Texas area. For many years, they would continue to fly me in to speak at the camps. I also had the privilege of holding a camp in Haiti for a couple of years.

As I look back over my ministry, the Lord has certainly blessed me through the bible schools and camps. These days, when I get to speak or attend large gatherings of pastors and full-time ministry folks, it seems that there are so many times when someone will approach me and say, "Bro. Bill, do you remember me? I was saved or surrendered to full-time work at one of the camps you spoke at." They are all grown up now and continue to do the work I can no longer do. I would have to say that children's programs like the bus ministry, vacation bible schools, and youth camps have been some of the most fruitful and rewarding times of my life.

My motto has always been if you want to be young, stay around kids. If you want to feel old, try to keep up with them! *Are you kidding me?* That's probably the reason I've lived to be 85! My grandkids call me *Magic Grandpa* and still tell me I'm a kid at heart. I hope that's true.

Chapter 48

GUEST SPEAKERS

I'VE HOSTED SEVERAL GUEST speakers during my ministry. Among them was J.C. Sullivan, the get-away driver for Bonnie and Clyde. He was in prison when Bonnie and Clyde were killed. In answer to his mother's prayers, he went to a revival meeting and was gloriously saved and later built the Nu-way starch and bleach company that netted millions of dollars throughout the United States.

I heard our local television station in Dodge City, Kansas was soon going to air the film *Bonnie and Clyde*. I contacted the station manager, Wendell Elliott, and said I wanted to buy advertisement time before and after the movie, inviting the viewers to come and hear the get-away driver for Bonnie and Clyde the next Sunday morning. Sunday evening, we showed a film from J.C. Sullivan's life story. He had certainly changed into a true man of God.

Max Palmer was an 8'2" giant who was featured in one of the *Planet of the Apes* movies and TV wrestling. When I walked down the street with him, he was head and shoulders above me. His TV career came to an end when they couldn't depend upon him because of his alcoholism. A great day came in his life when he repented of his sin and trusted Jesus. After that, it seemed he witnessed to most people he met, wanting them to meet the same Lord that freed him from sin.

Another guest speaker was Richard Miller. He had been born with no arms and legs. Even with the daily challenges, Richard completed college with a law degree. He was married and had two young children. It was remarkable, the things he could do. He had a motor home custom made so he was able to drive it. We rented the Junior High Auditorium in Dodge

THE BEST IS YET TO COME

City, Kansas and had the largest attendance we had ever had. Over 800 people came to hear Bro. Richard Miller's great testimony of God's saving grace.

One very memorable meeting was with the evangelist, Joe Boyd, who was an all-American football player. Bro. Boyd was also a powerful preacher and a great soul winner! One day, while he was holding a meeting for us in Bremerton, Washington, I took Bro. Boyd out soul winning and took him by the home of Ted and Jean Balter, a family I had met before and invited to church. As we walked to the door, we could hear that Ted was watching a football game. So when he answered, I said, "Ted, let me introduce you to an all-American football player who was listed in the *Sports Illustrated* 25th *Anniversary Edition* as one of the best football players of all time!" Ted readily invited us in the house, and we sat down on the couch. Within fifteen or twenty minutes, Bro. Boyd asked Ted, "If you died today, do you know you would go to heaven?" Ted replied, "I'd like to think I would." Bro. Boyd then spent several minutes letting him know how he could be sure. The next thing I knew, Ted was on his knees giving his life to Jesus! After we left, Ted told his wife to get ready because they were going to the revival that night. At the altar call, Ted surrendered his life to Jesus and was baptized that night. He faithfully served for six years before going home to be with the Lord on October 3, 1999. He loved the Lord and the Westside Baptist Church.

When we were in Dodge City, we had many other great pastors and evangelists including Art Wilson, Al Wells, and Bob Smith. And then, in Bremerton, Washington we had Tom Williams, Carl Hatch, and many others.

Since being ordained sixty-eight years ago, I could never list all of the souls that were saved and lives that were changed—some of them during these special meetings with great evangelists. The Lord knows and to God be the glory, great things he hath done!

Bro. Bill and Norma Wambsganss, 1990

Bro. Bill, Evelyn Musgrove, Leon Wambsganss,
Eleanor Wambsganss, 1994

Bro. Bill, (1996)

Ralph and Sharon Bates (Children: Sheree' and Brian)

Bro. Bill and Sharon Wambsganss, 1996

Bro. Bill and Grandson Keith Bates in Haiti, 1997

Bro. Bill and siblings, Evelyn, Leon, Paul, and mother, Eleanor (1999)

Colorado Youth Camp, 2001

Texas Youth Camp, 2003

Grandpa and Grandson, Landon Methvin, 2007

EPILOGUE:
LOOKING THROUGH THE
REARVIEW MIRROR

Brethren, I count not myself to have apprehended:
but this one thing I do, forgetting those things which
are behind, and reaching forth unto those things which are
before, I press toward the mark for the prize of the high
calling of God in Christ Jesus.

(PHILIPPIANS 3:13-14)

ALL MY LIFE I'VE HAD AN INTEREST in cars and one of the greatest parts of a car is the rearview mirror. As I look back over my 85 years, there have been so many happy memories. Only God could have planned such a life! He's been with me all the way through and, after every storm, he's brought a rainbow. He's led me over every mountain top and through the deepest valleys—through the joy of a new baby being born and the tears at an open grave. God has been there through it all.

But as it is written, Eye hath not seen, nor ear heard, neither
have entered into the heart of man, the things which God hath
prepared for them that love him. **(I CORINTHIANS 2:9)**

My prayer is that this book will help lead someone to a closer walk with God, or maybe even lead someone to know the Lord as their personal Savior. I would like to leave you with the plan of salvation:

For all have sinned and come short of the glory of God . . .

(ROMANS 3:23)

But God commendeth his love toward us, in that, while we were yet sinners, Christ died for us. **(ROMANS 5:8)**

For the wages of sin is death; but the gift of God is eternal life through Jesus Christ our Lord. **(ROMANS 6:23)**

That if thou shalt confess with thy mouth the Lord Jesus, and shalt believe in thine heart that God hath raised him from the dead, thou shalt be saved. For with the heart man believeth unto righteousness; and with the mouth confession is made unto salvation. **(ROMANS 10:9-10)**

For whosoever shall call upon the name of the Lord shall be saved. **(ROMANS 10:13)**

The Lord is not slack concerning his promise, as some men count slackness; but is longsuffering to us-ward, not willing that any should perish, but that all should come to repentance. **(II PETER 3:9)**

The theme of the whole Bible is summed up in Isaiah 1:18:

Come now, and let us reason together, saith the Lord: though your sins be as scarlet, they shall be as white as snow; though they be red like crimson, they shall be as wool.

Thank God for giving us his only begotten son to die on the cross as the Lamb of God, to shed his precious blood for the payment of our sin.

Therefore be ye also ready: for in such an hour as ye think not the Son of man cometh. **(MATTHEW 24:44)**

Will you be ready to meet God? Are your family and friends ready?

What could be better than going to Heaven?

Going to Heaven and taking your family and friends with you!

PUBLISHER'S NOTE

THE LAST SECTION OF THIS BOOK was set aside to let readers know where Bro. Bill and the close family members he wrote of are. As the final touches were being made, the Legacy Press team learned of an important change of address for Brother Bill. He left his earthly home and quietly stepped into the final calling of his life—heaven.

We thought it was appropriate to repeat a line from these pages about how Bro. Bill felt about his life and his first moment in heaven:

> *When my time comes to die, I hope that I will have lived*
> *to please my dearest friend, my master and my Lord,*
> *Jesus Christ and not myself. I long to hear him say,*
> *"Well done good and faithful servant!"*

We believe Bro. Bill heard those words.

The memories shared in this book tell of a life well-lived and well-loved. It is our hope that as you read and cherish them, you'll be able to know with confidence that *the best is yet to come.*

ROBIN GRUNDER,
founder of Legacy Press

APPENDIX A

OBITUARY

WILLIAM RICHARD WAMBSGANSS

WILLIAM RICHARD WAMBSGANSS passed away on Sunday, October 18, 2020 in Cedar Park, Texas at eighty-five years of age. He was born on July 4, 1935 in Fall River, Kansas to George and Eleanor Wambsganss. He was born on a farm and lived there throughout his childhood. At the young age of five, William Richard received Christ as his personal Savior, changing the course of his life forever. In 1951, he surrendered to preach the gospel and was ordained at the age of sixteen, along with his father, who had also surrendered to the ministry.

At the age of eighteen, "Bro. Bill" as he was then called, started working at the Wichita Baptist Tabernacle as an intern and met his first love, Norma Luella Smith. A year later, they were married. During this time, Bro. Bill accepted his first pastorate at Bible Baptist Church in Eureka, Kansas. The majority of his ministry was spent pastoring two churches: The Bible Baptist Church in Dodge City, Kansas for twenty-two years and The Westside Baptist Church in Bremerton, Washington for twenty years.

In 1994, after being married for thirty-eight years, the love of his life, Norma, died and went to heaven while he was pastoring in Bremerton. Bro. Bill met Sharon Bates, the widow of a pastor friend, and they fell in love and married in 1995. Bro. Bill always said Sharon was his second blessing. They ministered in Bremerton for seven more years after they were married.

After Bro. Bill retired from the ministry at the age of 67, he continued to do evangelism for the next decade. Sharon and Bro. Bill were married for almost twenty-two years when she died on December 11, 2016.

Bro. Bill spent the last four years of his life living in Texas with his daughter, Becky Lewis, where he attended Heritage Baptist Church in Georgetown, Texas. He loved spending three hours a day praying for everyone on his very long prayer list. Bro. Bill also just finished writing his first book and hoped it would be a blessing to all his friends and family.

William Richard Wambsganss is survived by his six children: Rebecca Lewis of Leander, Texas, Bonnie LaVielle (husband Bill) of Garland, Texas, Brenda Rabe (husband, Mark) of Fate, Texas, Bill Wambsganss of Rowlett, Texas, Beth Wambsganss of Rowlett, Texas, and Betty Methvin (husband Edward) of Rowlett, Texas. He was also survived by his step-children: Brian Bates (wife Leslie) of Florence, Colorado and Sheree' Bates of Airway Heights, Washington. Bro. Bill has twenty-one grandchildren and forty-nine great-grand-children, as well as many nieces, nephews, and hosts of friends.

TRIBUTES

Written on October 18, 2020
by granddaughter-in-law,
Allison LaVielle

It was an exciting day in Heaven,
A believer was coming home!
He spent his whole life preaching,
But not with words alone.

Bro. Bill lived out the gospel,
And told everyone he could.
If someone didn't know God's love,
After meeting him they would!

He wasn't worried about recognition,
Or being praised for his works.
His goal in life was to show the world,
How we should be the church.

He raised an amazing family,
Just one example of God's grace.
Many years they spent together,
Singing and teaching all over the place!

When your heart is full of Jesus,
There's no way to hold it in.
Bro. Bill just wanted the world to know
God's love and mercy covers every sin!

There's not one thing in this life you could do,
That would put you out of reach.
Each life is sacred and special,
That's why he dedicated his to preach.

He knew his time was not his own,
That we are only passing through.
And he used each waking hour he had
To show others how God loves you!

A void is left down here on earth,
Among everyone he knew.
We will miss him so and our hearts will ache,
But one thing we know is true.

Bro. Bill isn't gone in any way,
Besides on earth in flesh.
He's alive and well with Jesus
Complete . . . healthy . . . and refreshed!

He's been waiting for his day in Heaven,
What a joy he must be feeling.
He's experiencing all the things he longed for;
He's now received complete healing!

We'll miss him so—the laughs, the pranks,
The Bible stories and songs.
The magic tricks, the poems he wrote,
The prayers he prayed all day long.

But we know we'll see him soon again,
And until then I know it's true.
Bro. Bill would want us to spread the Word,
Tell the world that Jesus loves You!

We love you Magic Grandpa.

Written on October 19, 2020
by granddaughter, ShaReé LaVielle Harris

M Y GRANDPA, BRO. BILL WAMBSGANSS, lived a selfless life. He asked Jesus into his heart when he was five, and he later surrendered his life into the ministry. He truly lived his life to tell others about Christ.

In the summer, my sisters, Shauna Tobin and Sonia Dorsey, along with my cousin, Jeremy Rabe, would make the trip from Texas to Washington State to live with our grandparents for the summer. It was during those summer days that we observed our grandparents' ministry.

We saw my grandpa rise early every morning (he thought it was a sin to sleep in), off to win souls for the Lord. Even on Saturday after bus breakfast, he would take us out on bus visitation where he would visit with sick and elderly members of his congregation, or he would witness door-to-door. When I was little, I hated this. Not everyone he witnessed to looked nice or even smelled nice, but grandpa said everyone deserved the right to know Jesus.

My grandpa only rested one day a week. On Sundays, between morning and evening service, he would take a nap. But the rest of the week he was constantly on the go, working and giving to others.

One night during the summer, grandpa and grandma took us to a Seattle Mariners' game and, sure enough, grandpa brought tracts for us to pass out at the game. I was so embarrassed that I left my tracts on the bathroom counter after placing one in each stall. Now as an adult, I'm ashamed and it's my hope that at least one of those tracts was read.

At every family function, we always begged grandpa to tell us a Bible story. He often preached at youth camps and his Bible stories were legendary. Grandpa would proudly tell his story, but he would always end the same way. He would look around at each family member and he would say, "When we all get to heaven and we are seated around the table as a family, I want to look around and not see one empty chair." He wants all of his children, grandchildren, and great-grandchildren seated around that table with him.

I'm so thankful and grateful for my childhood. I think anyone who knows our family can see the influence of my grandpa and grandma in each one of us. It is my hope that I live a selfless, hard working life and love the Lord like my grandpa did.

Written on October 20, 2020
by grandson, Keith Bates

OUR LOSS IS HEAVEN'S GAIN! We have been blessed with such amazing grandparents. Grandpa Wambsganss preached my ordination and was one of my great, special influencers and mentors. We adore this special grandfather and want to share some lessons learned from him. These weren't spoken as much as they were lived out before us.

† Never pass an ice cream shop. Stop and have a cone.

† Love and be faithful to your wife.

† Napkins and the back of receipts are great places to write sermon notes.

† Make your children sing together; it knits their hearts together their whole life long.

† Don't send your kids to Sunday school. Get out of bed and take them!

† Never keep what you can give away.

† If you enter my home, you are no longer homeless or alone in the world. You have a family now.

† Keep a sweet spirit, especially to those unkind to you.

† Always speak well of others in their presence and their absence.

† Babies are a blank slate. You get to write who they become. Make it a tale worth reading.

† Kids are better than adults.

† Church camp is the best week of the year!

† There are no regrets when you live a holy life.

† Eat what you want. Just don't forget to take your insulin afterwards.

† Your children are a blessing. And grandkids are even better.

† Laugh at yourself whenever possible.

† Honor your parents and their memory.

† Finish Strong!

† A life lived for God is a life of untold blessings.

Written on December 9, 2020
by Mandy Wambsganss Walker, Granddaughter

GRANDPA, I HAVE SO MANY, MANY MEMORIES with you that I will cherish forever. Your love for our heavenly Father will continue to shine in my heart. As I look up at the sky I know you're watching over not just me, but many, many others. Everyone in your prayer book and even strangers you have passed on the streets. We will meet again when the Lord reunites us. I love you and will miss you so much. Tell Grandma I have missed her dearly and am glad she has you there now.

Written on December 9, 2020
by Brenda Rabe, daughter

WHAT A LUCKY GIRL I AM. Blessed with the most Amazing Parents! I am reminded of the song, "We must love them while we can". That is so true! Time just seems to hurry on and the days turn into years. The moments that we have soon disappears. I feel like I am the richest girl in town! It has nothing to do with money.

I love you dad! Thank you so much for giving us the family legacy that we all will strive to live up to.

Your favorite daughter….Brenda

Written on December 9, 2020
by Bill Wambsganss, son

I'M SO THANKFUL TO HAVE HAD such a Godly father. He studied and preached the word of God his entire life. But the thing that impacted me the most was being able to witness how he showed the love of God on a daily basis and I'll always remember that. From working on cars to teaching me right from wrong, he was always there. He always led by example and pointed me in the right direction. I wouldn't have survived living in a house of six women without my Dad.

Written on December 9, 2020
by Beth Wambsganss, daughter

MY DAD WAS ONE OF A KIND! He was selfless, kind-hearted, magical, loving, funny, generous and mischievous! Life will not be the same without him. We love and miss you dad!!!

Written on December 8, 2020
by Betty Methvin, daughter

I STARTED THINKING AND WRITING DOWN some of the best attributes and memories of our sweet dad, and the one that kept coming to mind was dad's heart. Our dad had the biggest heart ever. On numerous occasions throughout our lives, dad would give his very last dime to someone in need.

There was a one time in Dodge City, Kansas and we had just sit down to eat lunch. We lived right next door to the church in the parsonage. A lady came to the door and said her family needed food. Dad said, "You're just in time", He then told us kids to get our lunch bagged up for this stranger's family. After the lady left, our mom said, "We really don't have anything else to eat." Dad responded, "Well, praise the Lord, that's when you know you are doing the Lord's will. If we had plenty, it wouldn't be a sacrifice." Guess what, dad was 100% right!

Through the years, time and time again, God always supplied all of our needs. If my dad wouldn't have given away all of our food or given our very last dime, we would never have realized God's miraculous faithfulness. By the way, we never went hungry. Our mom had a way of cooking something out of nothing and we thought it was a feast.

Written on October 29, 2020
by Josh Rabe, grandson

I HAD THE PRIVILEGE OF CALLING WILLIAM WAMBSGANSS, my grandpa. I remember taking trips to Washington for the summer when I was young to see grandpa and grandma. We would walk up and down the hill from the parsonage to the church to hear him preach. He had a passion for God, people, service and giving that inspires me to this day.

I've never seen someone so willing to do so much for others, while putting his own needs to the side. I usually played baseball during the summers, so I didn't get to see them every summer but I would often get to visit with him. He came to Texas to visit one time and he told me to get my baseball glove and we walked down the street to a park that had a backstop. We started playing catch. I will say this, he tried really hard, but he wasn't very good at it. Needless to say, we were playing and the balls would go behind him, hit him in the arm, hit him in the legs and he would just keep getting the ball and throwing it back to me. He never complained about it and he wouldn't quit until I was ready to stop. He always put others needs above his own.

Grandpa was a patient man, it took a lot to get under his skin, but I could do it. I remember when I was young, my cousin Dallas, grandpa and I went to the store. Dallas and I got along most of the time, but this day we were really at each other's throats, pushing and shoving each other. Grandpa had told us to stop fighting and we wouldn't stop. I ended up hitting Dallas hard and Grandpa came up beside me and tapped me on the side of my head. It caught me off guard, since it was icy outside I ended up falling down. Grandpa helped me up. We all got in the car, everyone was very quiet on the way home. When we got home, before we got out of the car grandpa turned around and started praying. He prayed for Dallas and I and the whole situation and how he responded to it. I knew he prayed a lot and he had prayed with me before. But that day it hit home what a man of prayer he was.

When I grew up and had a family of my own, I was so grateful that my wife and kids got to know him and see what a godly man he was. I can still remember my kids loving to see grandpa over the holidays and seeing him do his magic tricks. They called him magic grandpa. He would gather all the kids around him and tell Bible stories, do magic tricks and entertain them. He had a way of connecting with the kids and wanting to share the gospel with them any way he could.

My Grandpa was a wonderful man of faith and service. I love you Grandpa.

Written on December 8, 2020
by daughter, Bonnie Wambsganss LaVielle

ICOULD NOT EVEN BEGIN TO TELL you the great influence my Mom and Dad had in my life. My Mom was the one we would go to with everything. She was a nurturer and we had daily conversations. She taught me how to be a Godly wife and mother. After my Mom died, Dad became my rock. I didn't realize until Dad moved to Texas four years ago how similar we are. Dad's mind was always going, it never stopped. He had months planned out with things he would like to do. I'm the same way. I have weekly, monthly and yearly to-do lists. The difference is, my Dad's were all about spiritual things. His lists were about praying for people, ministry, helping others. Very few of the things on his lists were about personal items.

I really believe I've learned more from my Dad in these last four years, than I've learned the rest of my life. My Dad's main goal in life was to lead others to Jesus. EVERYTHING he did was to try and make that happen. He never had an unkind word, was always so pleasant. Dad had a way of calming you down. If I had a bad day, all I needed to do is call my Dad. Not hearing his voice again and hearing him say, PRAISE THE LORD again will be the hardest thing.

During my Dad's entire life, he looked at the positive in everything and he always knew God was in control. If we had a flat tire on the highway with all six of us kids in the car, the first words out of his mouth would be, "Praise the Lord!" And he meant that! We would immediately have prayer and thank the Lord for his protection.

What a heritage to leave your family! My Dad was and is my hero and I cherish the time God gave him to us on this earth. I hope to carry on his great love of the Lord and people until I see him again!

A tribute to the Best Dad in the World
from Becky Lewis

A LARGE FAMILY IS SUCH a BLESSING from God! Dad had a big family….his children, grandchildren and great-grandchildren were his delight. The past four years, they had a huge role in his life, and he loved and prayed for all of them daily.

During these four years it was my privilege to share my home and life with Dad. My siblings and I felt it would be best for Dad to come to Texas to live, so we could spoil him. Two weeks after his wife Sharon passed away, we brought him to Texas. He left the places, people and churches he loved and had pastored and ministered to for the last thirty-plus years. He only came with a couple of suitcases and a big smile. Dad went from being the care-giver to being in my home where I took over that role. He graciously accepted it. He couldn't drive due to his poor eye-sight so my friends became his friends and my church family became his church family. They loved him and treated him with such honor. It had to be very difficult giving up so much of his independence, but you would never have known it.

My dad had joy like I've never experienced before. His joy came from his Lord and Savior and it was real. He spent all day while I worked, reading (listening), to his Bible. He prayed at least three hours a day. When I went to bed at night I would hear him praying and as I woke up in the morning, he was praying.

My Dad has always been my hero, but to get to see him in every situation at the end of his life display joy and thankfulness, has impacted my life more than I could ever express. I love you Dad and I wish I could have at least four more years with you. I am so thankful we'll spend eternity together.

APPENDIX B

WHERE WE ARE TODAY—BLESSED BEYOND MEASURE!!!

WAMBSGANSS FAMILY:

BECKY LEWIS

Becky Lewis lives in Leander, Texas. Becky has two sons with her first husband, Jim Fowler, who died in 1990. Becky's second husband, Dwayne Lewis, died October 2, 2011. Dwayne has one daughter. All three kids live close to Becky. The joy of Becky's life are her seven grandkids. Becky is very active in Heritage Baptist Church in Georgetown, Texas.

BONNIE LaVIELLE

Bonnie and Bill LaVielle are retired and live in Garland, Texas. They are very active in New Liberty Baptist Church, where Bill serves as a deacon. They have four children and eleven grandchildren. Bill and Bonnie thank the Lord that all of their kids and grandkids live close to them. They enjoy spending time with their family more than anything else.

BRENDA RABE

Brenda and Mark Rabe live in Royse City, Texas and go to church at New Liberty Baptist Church. Brenda has three sons and nine grandchildren. Everywhere Brenda goes, she is the life of the party! Mark is retired, and Brenda works for the YMCA and has for almost thirty years. Brenda and her sisters still sing together in church and at other events.

BILL WAMBSGANSS

Bill lives in Rowlett, Texas. He has three kids and eight grandkids. Bill is a supervisor with The Coca-Cola Company. Recently, he bought a small house on thirty-eight acres outside of Dallas. He is looking forward to spending time at Pappy's Ranch in the country with his family.

BETH WAMBSGANSS

Beth lives in Rowlett, Texas. Beth has worked for the YMCA for thirty years. She is also a second mom for all of her nieces and nephews. In particular, Beth is Landon Methvin's surrogate mother. Beth is our nurturer and is so giving. She attends New Liberty Baptist Church with her siblings.

BETTY JO METHVIN

Betty Jo and Edward Methvin have three children and live in Rowlett, Texas. They also have two grandchildren. Landon, their fifteen-year-old son, has Down Syndrome. Landon is the joy of everyone's life. You can't be around Landon and not be happy. Betty Jo is a realtor and Edward works for The Coca-Cola Company. Betty has a beautiful voice and is often asked to sing for churches in the Dallas area.

BATES FAMILY

SHEREÉ BATES

Sharon's daughter, Shereé, bought the Bates's family home in Airway Heights, Washington, where Sharon and Bro. Bill lived until Sharon passed away. Shereé is a writer and spends much of her time with her very-much-loved dogs, writing. Shereé enjoys spending time with her three children and two grandchildren who live fairly close to her.

BRIAN BATES

Sharon's son, Brian, and his wife, Leslie, live in Penrose, Colorado. They have three children and thirteen grandchildren. Brian and Leslie attend the church that their son, Keith Bates, pastors in Penrose. They are both retired and love traveling to the beach and spending time with their grandchildren.

BROTHER BILL'S SIBLINGS

LEON'S FAMILY

Leon died on March 30, 2020. His wife, Becky Wambsganss, lives in Southlake, Texas. She and Leon had three sons before Leon passed away. Her son, Stephen, lives in Friday Harbor, Washington and has one daughter, Caitlyn Bowman. Andrew and his wife Leigh live in Southlake, Texas with their two sons. Phillip and his wife Tiffani live in Mansfield, Texas with their three children.

EVELYN'S FAMILY

Evelyn Musgrove died on December 13, 2006. Carl Musgrove lives in Independence, Kansas with his wife, Joycelyn. Combined, they have eight kids and eleven grandkids. Joycelyn is retired from Independence Community College where she met Evelyn and was a good friend of Evelyn's before she died.

PAUL'S FAMILY

Paul Wambsganss died on March 24, 2008. He and his wife, Marsha, had two children, Trisha and Aaron. Sadly, Aaron passed away on April 19, 2019 from a freak accident at work. He was such a fine young man and Paul and Marsha were very proud of him. Trisha lives with her mother in Wichita, Kansas, where they are very active in their church.

APPENDIX C

FAMILY TREES

1. Wambsganss Family: George and Eleanor

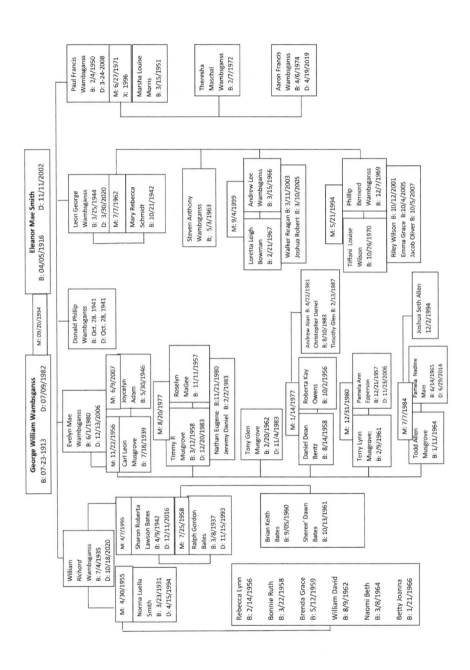

2. Wambsganss Family: William and Norma

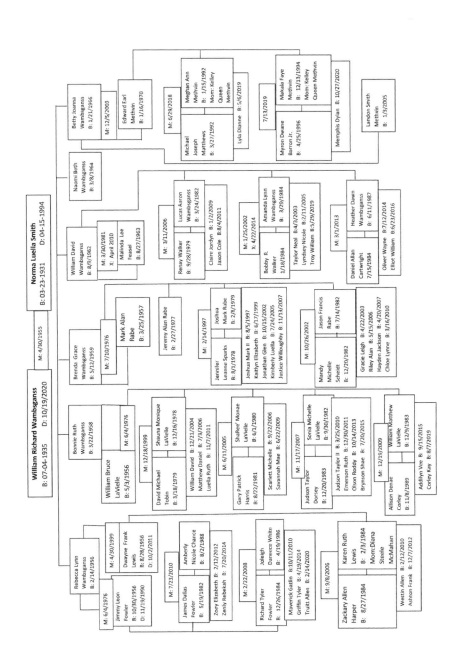

3. Bates Family Tree

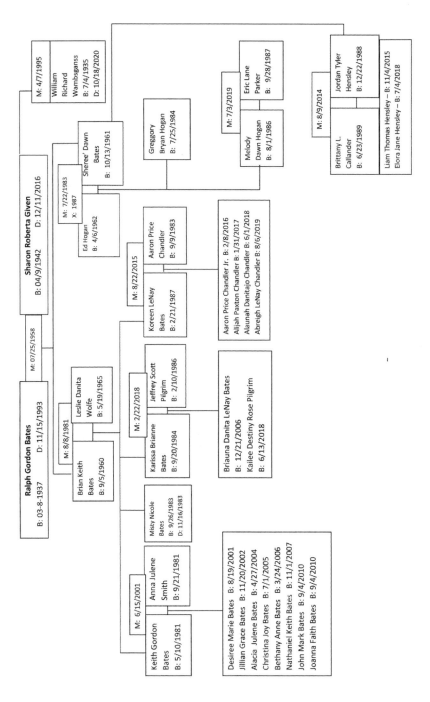

Ralph Gordon Bates
B: 03-8-1937   D: 11/15/1993

Sharon Roberta Given
B: 04/9/1942   D: 12/11/2016

M: 07/25/1958

M: 4/7/1995
William Richard Wambsganss
B: 7/4/1935
D: 10/18/2020

Sheree' Dawn Bates
B: 10/13/1961

M: 7/22/1983
X: 1987
Ed Hogan
B: 4/6/1962

Greggory Bryan Hogan
B: 7/25/1984

M: 7/3/2019
Eric Lane Parker
B: 9/28/1987

Melody Dawn Hogan
B: 8/1/1986

M: 8/9/2014
Jordan Tyler Hensley
B: 12/22/1988

Brittany L. Callander
B: 6/23/1989

Liam Thomas Hensley – B: 11/4/2015
Elora Jane Hensley – B: 7/4/2018

M: 8/8/1981
Leslie Danita Wolfe
B: 5/19/1965

Brian Keith Bates
B: 9/5/1960

M: 8/22/2015
Aaron Price Chandler
B: 9/9/1983

Koreen LeNay Bates
B: 2/21/1987

Aaron Price Chandler Jr. B: 2/8/2016
Alijah Paxton Chandler B: 1/31/2017
Alaunah Danitajo Chandler B: 6/1/2018
Abreigh LeNay Chandler B: 8/6/2019

M: 2/22/2018
Jeffrey Scott Pilgrim
B: 2/10/1986

Karissa Brianne Bates
B: 9/20/1984

Briauna Danita LeNay Bates
B: 12/21/2006
Kailee Destiny Rose Pilgrim
B: 6/13/2018

Misty Nicole Bates
B: 9/26/1983
D: 11/16/1983

M: 6/15/2001
Anna Julene Smith
B: 9/21/1981

Keith Gordon Bates
B: 5/10/1981

Desiree Marie Bates   B: 8/19/2001
Jillian Grace Bates   B: 11/20/2002
Alacia Julene Bates   B: 4/27/2004
Christina Joy Bates   B: 7/1/2005
Bethany Anne Bates   B: 3/24/2006
Nathaniel Keith Bates   B: 11/1/2007
John Mark Bates   B: 9/4/2010
Joanna Faith Bates   B: 9/4/2010

171

Made in the USA
Las Vegas, NV
18 January 2021